A LOOK AT Learie Constantine

Undine Giuseppi

Nelson

Acknowledgements

The author and publishers wish to thank the following for the use of copyright material:
Aldus Books Ltd for lines from *English Cricket* by Neville Cardus from BRITAIN IN PICTURES series published Collins 1947; Clarendon Press for lines from *Forefathers* by Edmund Blunden; Jonathan Cape Limited for lines from *Good Days* by Neville Cardus; Harper & Row Publishers Inc. for lines from *Incident* from ON THESE I STAND by Countee Cullen; Hutchinson Publishing Group for extracts from *Cricketers Carnival* and *Cricket in the Sun* by Learie Constantine; Mr Peter Newbolt for an extract from *Vitai Lampada* by Sir Henry Newbolt (from POEMS OLD AND NEW); Gordon Bell for an extract from *Wayside Sketches*; Thanks are also due to the following for the use of photographs: Central Press, pp 4, 124; Colorsport, p i; Paul Popper, pp 79, 94; Syndication International, p 115; Topix, p 128; Mrs Gloria Valere, cover, pp 24, 31, 38, 52, 105; 'The Sun' Feature Bureau, Sydney, p 60; 'The Trinidad Guardian' for the photograph of the author on the back cover.

Thomas Nelson and Sons Ltd
36 Park Street, London W1Y 4DE
P.O. Box 27 Lusaka
P.O. Box 18123 Nairobi
77 Coffee Street, San Fernando, Trinidad

Thomas Nelson (Australia) Ltd
597 Little Collins Street, Melbourne 3000

Thomas Nelson and Sons (Canada) Ltd
81 Curlew Drive, Don Mills, Ontario

Thomas Nelson (Nigeria) Ltd
P.O. Box 336 Apapa, Lagos

First published 1974
ISBN 0 17 566177 4

Printed in Great Britain

Contents

To MY GRANDSON WARREN but for whom this book would have been finished long ago; and to MY HUSBAND NEVILLE who rendered me invaluable assistance when the publishers' deadline loomed large

Introduction

To produce a mighty book, you must choose a mighty theme.

Moby Dick Herman Melville

This should be a mighty book. The mighty theme has been chosen; the will to make it one is there. If only that were all!

Learie Constantine, the subject of this biography, was a versatile man. During his sixty-nine year span of life he was, among other things, cricketer, lawyer, politician, lecturer, author. A mighty theme indeed! But it is chiefly the last-mentioned facet of his versatility – author – that now makes difficult the production of a mighty book, with him as the theme.

His published works include *Cricket and I*, *Cricket in the Sun*, *How to Play Cricket*, *Cricketers' Carnival*, *Cricket Crackers*, *Colour Bar, and The Young Cricketer's Companion.* He also wrote for leading magazines and newspapers in England.

In his many books he has told much about himself. There is little which is new that is left to tell – certainly, where cricket is concerned, that is so. It is almost inevitable that, as page follows page, many readers will be able to say, "I have heard that one before." Yes, whatever is worth telling, Constantine has told it himself somewhere.

In doing research for this biography, I have read every book that Learie himself has written. I have read all that I could come across that has been written about him. I have talked with his relatives and with his friends, and often I, too, have found myself saying, "I have heard that one before."

I have talked with his admirers, and even with his detractors when I could find them. The greatest fault that the latter group could find in him was his tendency to give credit where credit was due. For often it was due to himself.

Learie made no apologies for this seeming weakness. In his first book *Cricket and I*, he quotes a eulogy of himself which was written by his collaborator C. L. R. James, and appeared in a Trinidad newspaper early in 1930 during the M.C.C. Tour.

"I make no apology for quoting here a eulogy of myself," he states, "since the title-page proclaims the egotism of this volume."

No one who has read his books, or who knew him personally, can say, however, that Learie told only of his successes. No one has related more stories about his failures than he himself has done. But such failures in no way detract from the impact which he made on those who saw him on the cricket field. Learie was by common consent rated among the six best fieldsmen in the world.

Louis Palgrave, in his *History of Surrey Cricket: 1902–1948*, describing the last Test match of the 1939 series played between England and the West Indies at the Oval, stated that Constantine fielded in his best style.

He continued, "If you never saw Constantine fielding at his best, it would be quite hopeless to try to describe it for you, but he almost discounted the usually accepted fact that it is impossible for a man to be in two places at the same time."

Others have stated that Constantine often did the impossible, and Ellis ('Puss') Achong, who played cricket with him, asserts that not only did he perform the impossible, but he also expected others to do the impossible too.

'Puss' tells the story of how on one occasion he was fielding at third slip. Learie was bowling and the batsman hit the ball towards gully. Learie shouted, "Get it, Achong," and was evidently quite disappointed because the latter, knowing how impossible such a feat would have been for him or any other normal human being, failed even to make the effort.

"Why didn't you catch it?" asked Learie seriously.

'Puss' looked at him calmly. "In case you don't know it," he replied, "there is only one Learie Constantine."

Cricket was Constantine's whole life. Beneath the façade of the lawyer, or the diplomat, the cricketer Learie was there. And even when his active cricketing days were done, in fancy he played many a match with a team chosen by himself.

"Perhaps, if I ever win my way to Olympus, they will level out a pitch of perfect turf within a hallowed field, and we shall play that game out." This is what he wrote towards the end of his book *Cricket in the Sun*.

And *Cricketers' Carnival* carries on the theme. In his imagination he has crossed over to the other side. But still, in fancy, he plays the game high on Mount Olympus, the dwelling-place of the gods.

What greater tribute can a biographer pay to such a man now

that he has actually 'crossed the Bar', than to set him once more on the field as he longed to be, where he may play again to his heart's content? Perhaps, from somewhere over there, as he sits in the Great Pavilion, he, too, may pause for a while, and pure fantasy though much of the opening chapters may be, he may read and enjoy this book, as I hope that you will.

Does the listener tire of hearing the same tune played over and over again, even though there may be some variations in the theme? Or does familiarity make a song more dear? This is for you to tell.

To those readers who may be familiar with the names of the cricketers who make up the imaginary team that I have set on Mount Olympus as Learie himself had set his team, it will be clear that I have chosen for the game only those players who, like him, have passed into the Beyond. If wicket-keepers in that game make more runs than those who were expert batsmen down here, and one wonders why, the answer is to be found in the Great Score Book kept by Life's Recording Angel.

I wish to thank all those kind persons who so willingly talked with me about Learie, and answered all my innumerable questions. Among such persons in Trinidad are Learie's daughter, Gloria Valere, his brother, Elias Constantine, and his cousin, Hubert Andrews; Hamilton Maurice, former President of the Senate of Trinidad and Tobago, C. Arnold Thomasos, Speaker of the House of Representatives of Trinidad and Tobago, Harold Duprés, a founder member of the P.N.M. Party, Ellis Achong, former West Indian Test cricketer, and Ellis' son-in-law, Mervyn Wong – 'a walking cricket encyclopedia'.

Special thanks are due to Leslie Jackson, the BBC Producer of the *This Is Your Life* programme, who gave me the opportunity to see the script; to Irving Rosenwater, who read and gave comments on the manuscript; and to John and Evelyn Kirk, who not only invited me to spend a weekend with them at their lovely home in Bolton, Lancashire, so that we could talk about Learie, but also took me, one fine Saturday afternoon, to Nelson. There I walked the streets where Learie walked, gazed at the house that had been 'home' for him, saw the sights that he had seen – the tall sycamore trees to the north-east, the chimney of the dye works hard by, Pendle Hill – the home of the Lancashire witches, the bowling green beyond the wall, and St Mary's Church tower in the distance. I admired the beautiful, level green grounds on which Learie had played (a cricket match was in progress then), and the old pavilion from which many a mighty cheer had risen in his honour. Then, crowning it all, was my meeting with the many friends that Learie had made in Nelson, friends whose smiles, and shining eyes, and eagerness to draw upon their memories of him for my benefit, revealed that after a quarter of a century almost, the magic of his personality was with them still.

Undine Giuseppi

1 Carnival dream fulfilled
(A fantasy)

For the field is full of shades
as I near the shadowy coast
And a ghostly batsman plays
to the bowling of a ghost.

At Lord's Francis Thompson

The mountain range stretched far away into the distance, peak towering upon peak, all like silent sentinels guarding the quiet valleys below. Darkly silhouetted against a paler sky, the tall trees merged into one.

Then Dawn brushed her lips across the face of Olympus. The darkness rolled away, and the sky became gradually brighter and brighter. The hills, the valleys, and the plains became more distinct. The stillness ceased. Birds sang in the trees, and sounds of renewed life could be heard everywhere. The Grecian gods were waking up.

Somewhere in the distance, the magnificent river Peneus, rising in Mount Pindus, flowed on from west to east, and together with a number of streams which joined it from the north and south, watered the whole countryside.

The widespread plain, with the dew still thick upon the grass, shone like a mass of sparkling diamonds scattered on some vast green sheet.

The chariot of the Sun, now clearly visible, continued to make its way across the sky, its golden rays devouring the shining dew.

It was Saturday, 10th July, 1971. Learie Constantine, dressed in immaculate cream flannels, and a new pair of white cricket boots, crossed the level green fields and joined the hundreds of cricketers and spectators already gathered there.

Cornflower blue skies above, and lush green grass below; tables laden with ice-cold drinks and delectable food – food fit for the gods! This was the scene that Learie joined – a scene made familiar because of his fantastic dream so many years before.

Cricketers, cricketers everywhere! Some known personally to Learie; he had played many a match with or against them! There were many others, too, whom he knew by reputation only.

From Australia, India, New Zealand, England, and from his own beloved West Indies they had come. And there was going to be a cricket festival – *Old Timers* versus his *Contemporaries*. What a carnival this would be for him!

"Carnival, says my dictionary, is solace of the body permitted in anticipation of any feast; or feasting or revelry in general."

Thus wrote Learie in his book *Cricketers' Carnival*. Then he continued, "But when I write my *Cricketers' Glossary*, a merry volume with which I propose to lighten mine old age, I shall explain the word otherwise: 'A cricket festival, on one of those splendid midsummer days one calls affectionately "a scorcher", when cricketers and the shades of cricketers gather to lie in the sun and watch twenty-two men out in the middle, and to talk all the old, spicy, nonsensical "shop" about the world's happiest game'."

Learie had known that the time would come when he must declare his 'first-class innings closed.' But, "I shall go on playing cricket somewhere, never fear," he wrote, "and I shall watch cricket even when I, who have been called 'Electric Heels', roll up to the turnstiles in nothing more electric than a bath-chair. Meanwhile, I propose to solace my body beforehand imagining my carnival."

Learie rubbed his eyes. Was he awake, or was he dreaming still? Here and there the details were different, but the basic pattern was the same.

Learie walked towards the pavilion, pausing for a moment here to greet one old friend, there to exchange banter with another.

From somewhere high up in the sky, there was a mighty sound of trumpets. The spectators in the stands saw Learie coming and rose to greet him. He acknowledged their cheers with a hearty grin and a huge wave of the hand. How happy he was to see so many of them there! And then it was that he saw his father and mother and brothers Ossie and Rodney among the crowd. His father was smiling approvingly. His mother, too, seemed pleased.

Learie looked down at his flannels – beautiful cream in colour, and as smartly creased as those of any of the rest of the players. In his mind, Learie went back through the years. He remembered his early days and the trouble he had had to acquire his first pair of flannels. His father had insisted that he should work for the money to buy them if he was to wear them. Working for a small salary, he had found it difficult to save much money, and it had taken him a long time to get them. Learie smiled at the memory.

Listed to play for *Old Timers* were Spofforth, Clem Hill, and Trumper of Australia; Ranjitsinhji, the dapper Indian prince; and from England, MacLaren, Jessop, Alfred Shaw, A. A. Lilley, Tom Richardson, Colin Blythe, and the bearded W. G. Grace, the

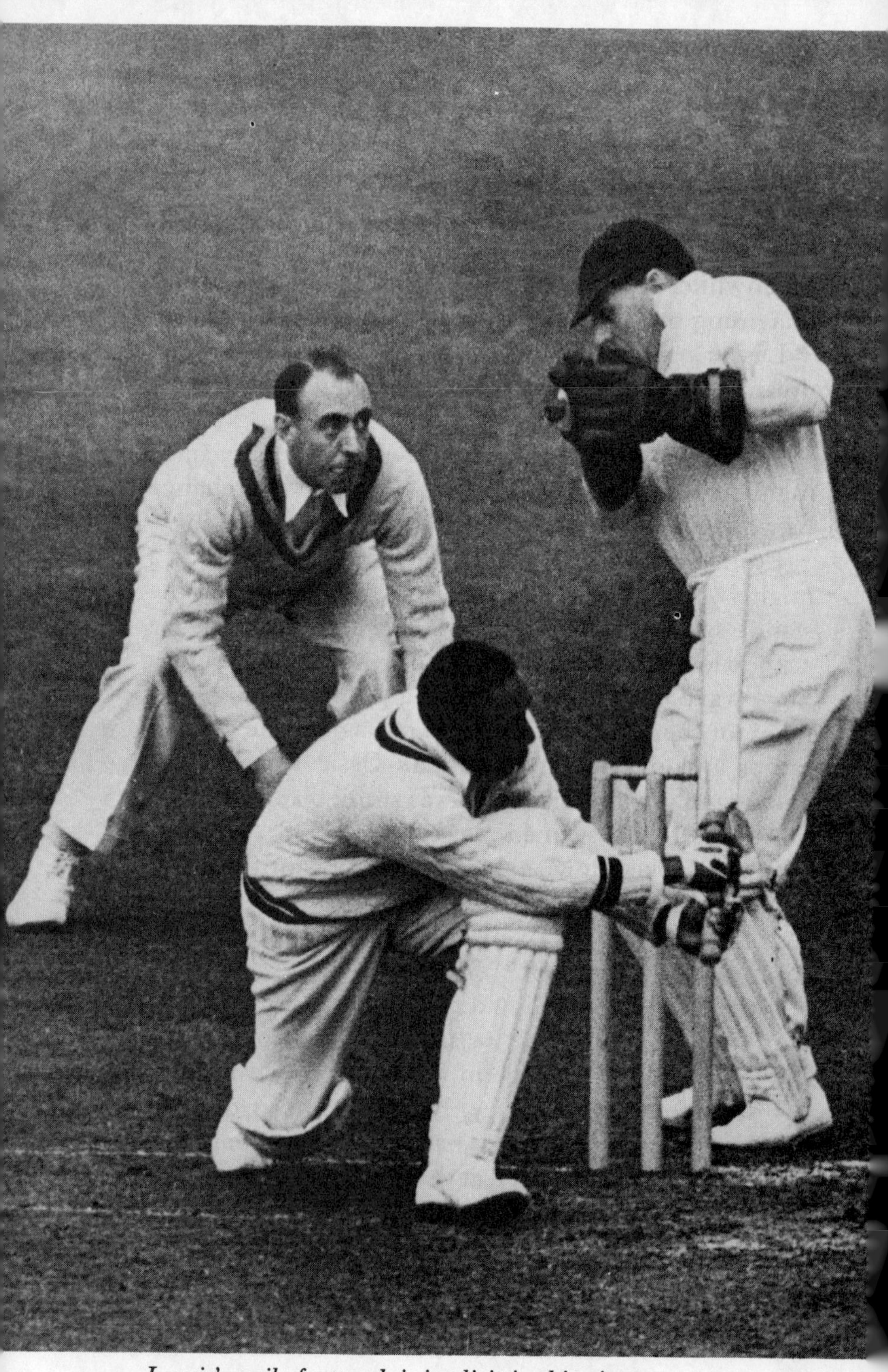

Learie's agile footwork is implicit in this picture of him sweeping to leg

Grand Old Man of cricket.

For *Contemporaries* were listed Hobbs, Hammond, Jardine, Rhodes, Larwood and Barnes from England; Ponsford, Bradman and Oldfield from Australia; and Headley and Constantine from the West Indies.

Learie scanned the pavilion for the members of his side. Skipper Jardine was there with a worried look on his face. Learie soon discovered why. The match was soon to begin, but Bradman, Headley, Larwood, Oldfield and Ponsford were not yet there.

"That's almost half the team," bemoaned Jardine. "What could have happened to them?"

Suddenly Learie knew. As if in a flash the answer came to him. Bradman and Headley and the others had not yet come across. They were still batting in a match somewhere down there. Learie missed their well-known faces.

There was a hasty scratching out of names, and an eager search for replacements. The game must go on.

Barnes came across to Jardine. "Blanckenberg is here. He would prefer to be a spectator only, but he is willing to play if you can't find anyone else," he said.

Learie opened his eyes in surprise. Blanckenberg was a South African whom Learie knew to be prejudiced against coloured people. Blanckenberg, whom he had succeeded as coach for Nelson, had once refused point blank to play in a match when he learned that Learie and Ellis ('Puss') Achong would be members of the team.

Learie turned to Jardine, and was about to suggest that the latter inform the South African that he, Learie, was scheduled to play in the match. Blanckenberg might want to withdraw his offer, Learie felt.

Just then, Blanckenberg came up and threw his arms around Learie's shoulders.

"Glad to see you, Learie," he said.

Learie's mouth fell open in surprise. This time he was sure he must be dreaming!

Blanckenberg smiled broadly.

"It's all right," he said. "I know better now. Over here we are all equals."

The approach of his uncle, Victor Pascall, saved Learie from whatever further embarrassment he might have felt.

Victor Pascall was his mother's brother, and he was an excellent slow bowler. Learie had had the privilege of playing intercolonial cricket with his father and Uncle Victor on the same team.

Victor Pascall turned to Jardine. "I knew of your predicament," he said, "and I have found four good cricketers for you."

Jardine was delighted.

"Who are they?" he inquired.

"The Australian all-rounders, McCabe and Gregory," Pascall replied, "McDonald, the Tasmanian bowler, and Cameron, the South African wicket-keeper."

"Another South African!" thought Learie. He would have preferred to see the Australian Wally Grout, but the choice of Cameron did not really matter so much. He had the reputation of being an excellent wicket-keeper batsman. And whatever might be thought of South Africans generally – Learie had reason to be grateful to at least one of them. That was Mr H. C. W. Johnson, who had given him a fairly good job at Trinidad Leaseholds, had taken great interest in his cricket, and had given him leave, whenever he wanted, on half-pay. When Learie finally left for England, Mr Johnson had assured him that a job would be there for him whenever he returned. Learie had felt then that neither in that world nor the next would he forget such generosity. He was grateful to him still.

There was one more replacement to be found.

"What about yourself?" Jardine questioned Pascall.

Victor shook his head. "One member of the family is enough," he said.

Someone (Learie was not sure who it was) pointed out to Skipper Jardine that Frank Worrell was there and suggested that he should be asked to play. He would undoubtedly be a great asset to any team.

Jardine nodded approvingly and turned to see where Frank was. There, stretched out on the soft, green turf was Frank, fast asleep, with a book beneath his head. He was young, but both Learie and Jardine knew that it would be good to have him play for their side.

Blanckenberg turned away, relieved that he was no longer needed.

"Good luck, Learie," he called, as he left.

Learie, the light of surprise still in his eyes, quietly watched him go.

Having got Frank to agree to play, Jardine was beside himself with glee. "We have a really good team," he said. "We'll knock the *Old Timers* all about." And then he whispered to Constantine, "When they go in to bat, don't forget to let them have some bodyline. You must scare the daylights out of them."

"What a match this will be!" thought Learie.

2 Prisoner at the Bar
(A fantasy continued)

"The strife is o'er, the battle done;
Now is the Victor's triumph won."

Translated from the Latin by Francis Pott

The teams as they lined up on Olympus were:

Old Timers	*Contemporaries*
(in order of batting)	
W. G. Grace (captain)	J. B. Hobbs
V. T. Trumper	W. Rhodes
K. S. Ranjitsinhji	F. M. Worrell
C. Hill	W. R. Hammond
A. C. MacLaren	S. J. McCabe
G. L. Jessop	D. R. Jardine (captain)
A. A. Lilley (wicket-keeper)	J. M. Gregory
A. Shaw	H. B. Cameron (wicket-keeper)
F. R. Spofforth	L. N. Constantine
T. Richardson	S. F. Barnes
C. Blythe	E. A. McDonald

Alec Skelding and Frank Chester, who had lost one arm in the war, were the umpires for the match. Before taking up his position on the field, Skelding looked carefully all around to ensure that there were no dogs about. He was scared of the creatures, as everyone knew.

W. G. Grace, the captain of *Old Timers*, won the toss, and went with Trumper to open the innings.

It was a keenly contested match. With six all-rounders on their side, *Contemporaries* appeared, on the surface, to have the edge on *Old Timers*. But no one could be certain of what would happen. Grace could hold his own against any bowler. On seventeen occasions he had carried his bat through an innings. And umpires' decisions did not bother him! Ranjitsinhji had the reputation of having hit 72 centuries in first-class cricket. More than that, he once made two separate centuries on the same day. Hill, the left-handed batsman, came from a cricketing family, and could be depended on to give a good account of himself. Jessop, the Croucher, was famous for hitting the ball, and hitting it hard. 157 in an hour was nothing to be scoffed at. Archie MacLaren, who had succeeded Grace as captain of England, once played an innings of 424 for Lancashire against Somerset and held this record for twenty-seven years. He was called the 'Sydney Wizard' because of his marvellous performances with the bat on that ground, and we are told that Australian umpires had been somewhat afraid to give him out, and usually settled doubtful decisions in his favour.

Fortunately for *Contemporaries*, neither Skelding nor Chester was an Australian.

Spectators took sides, and swapped stories of their heroes.

One *Old Timers'* backer – an Australian – predicted that Spofforth, 'the Demon', would wreak havoc in the ranks of *Contemporaries*. He related the story of how, in 1878, in a match between the M.C.C. and the Australians, Spofforth, taking over the bowling when England were 25 for 1, in 23 balls took 6 wickets for 4 runs. England, in that innings, were all out for 9 more runs.

"It was Spofforth who performed the first hat-trick

in the history of Test cricket," he reminisced proudly. "Three men out in three successive balls!"

"Don't forget Tom Richardson's four wickets in four successive balls," added another *Old Timers'* fan. "We'll skittle out *Contemporaries*!"

There was a loud guffaw.

"You have never heard of our opening bats, Hobbs and Rhodes, have you?" interjected a *Contemporaries'* backer. "I bet you they will be among the top scorers in this match. It is not for nothing that Surrey Club erected gates at the Oval in Hobbs' honour!"

Just then a loud shout rent the air. Constantine, following Jardine's instructions, had bowled a bumper at Grace. The latter, however, unperturbed, whacked it away with all his might, and with a taunting laugh, shouted at Learie, "That's what the bat is for."

At the end of *Old Timers'* first innings, they had scored 694 runs. The individual scores were: Grace 67, Trumper 37, Ranjitsinhji 60, Clem Hill 68, MacLaren 73, Jessop 81, Lilley 62, Shaw 64, Spofforth 73, Richardson 41, and Blythe 68.

The Recording Angel was seen checking the scoreboard against a little book he held in his hand. He smiled with a sense of satisfaction, as though he had something to do about determining the number of runs each player had scored. The sun stood still, as it had done on Gideon many long years before. The game continued.

Contemporaries went in to bat. Hobbs and Rhodes were among the top scorers, as had been predicted by a fan – Hobbs with 81, while Rhodes made 95. S. F. Barnes, the former Staffordshire bowler, amazed everyone with a score second only to Rhodes. He made 94 runs. No one, watching, could explain *how* it happened, but it *had* happened. Worrell, the famous West Indian all-rounder who had once scored 261 in a

Test match between the West Indies and England, made only 42 runs before he was stumped. The heavens shook as the gods mourned the fall of his wicket. Other scores were: Hammond 62, McCabe 58, Jardine 58, Gregory 77, Cameron 30, Constantine 69, and McDonald, struck by accident, 45. *Contemporaries'* first innings score was 711, a lead of 17 over *Old Timers*.

There was jollity among the teams as they relaxed, sipping ice-cold drinks all the while. The spectators stretched their legs. Lebrun Constantine and his wife Anna were surrounded by their friends who showered praises on Learie.

"How proud you must feel of your son!" they said.

Old Constantine's reply was muttered too softly for them to hear. "He is a Constantine," he said simply, as if that explained everything. He would talk to Learie when the match was over.

Old Timers went in to bat once more. W. G. Grace, to whom is attributed the honour of having made cricket England's national game, strode purposefully to the wicket. He would wipe out that deficit first, and then show *Contemporaries* what his side could do. No ill-feeling, mark you, but it was necessary to put them in their place.

Two sixes from his bat, and then a single! Trumper faces Barnes, and another single follows.

Out on the fields and in the stands, the spectators were still swapping tales.

"Did you hear the one about Chester?" one grey-haired old man asked.

He chuckled at the memory of the tale even before the telling of it.

"Tell us the story," persuaded the old man's

companions.

"He is the coolest one I know," began the raconteur. "Once, at the Oval, he gave out a famous visiting batsman l.b.w. The batsman was clearly annoyed about Chester's decision. He left the field, but in the pavilion later, he argued about it."

"And what happened?"

"Oh, he went up to Chester during the luncheon interval and asked him if he was quite sure of the decision, affirming that he wasn't really out."

"What did Chester say then?" urged on the old man's listeners.

The old man smiled.

"No?" Chester asked him, bending his head and raising his eyebrows. "Well, look in the evening papers, and you'll see that you *were* out."

The group chuckled.

"Had the batsman been a Barbadian," said one of them, with a teasing glance towards a group of West Indians standing nearby, "he would in all probability have glared at Chester, shaken his fist in the latter's face, and said, 'Ah could kill you!' "

There was a general outburst of laughter at the expense of Barbadians.

Meanwhile, the bowling has changed. Learie now holds the ball. Grace and Trumper are still there, Trumper facing Learie, and the score is 16. One more run to even up!

Learie bowls. It is a good ball, pitched middle and off, and just short of a length. Trumper, getting on the back foot, and playing as only Trumper can, guides the ball to the right of Worrell at gully.

In a flash Worrell is behind it and picks it up brilliantly. In a flash it is in Cameron's hands, but it is just too late to prevent a single. Grace has reached the crease in time. He faces Learie.

"Now to begin the second innings in earnest!" thinks Grace to himself.

But Constantine has had enough of Grace!

A ball with the power of seven devils behind it jumps up, and Grace pops it in front of him. The ball is in the air.

"What a pity the wicket-keeper is not close up! If point had not been quite so deep it might have been a catch!"

But stay! Like a bounding tiger Constantine comes down the pitch and the greatest catch in cricket history has been made.

"Neville Cardus should have been here to see this," thinks Learie, pleased. Years ago, at Lord's, when West Indies had played their first Test match in England, he had missed exactly such a catch off Larwood's bat. Cardus had written about that match for all the world to read.

There is a shout of astonishment and appreciation from the crowd. West Indian fans who had been standing on the fringe of the field, surge wildly forward, and invade the pitch. Hundreds and hundreds of them! They lift Learie shoulder high. There is mad scampering. The other cricketers all try to get to the safety of the pavilion. General confusion reigns!

Skelding lifts the bails and declares the day's entertainment closed.

"Lord's first," murmurs Learie in disbelief, remembering 1950, "and now the Olympian plains! Where next?"

He must wake up if this was a dream. But now he would never know how the game between *Old Timers* and *Contemporaries* would have ended!

And then suddenly the scene changed. It was a different place, a different time.

He stood, a prisoner at the Bar, while a solemn judge read out a list of charges to him.

"Learie Constantine, you are hereby charged that on various occasions during your sojourn elsewhere, you did wilfully and deliberately bowl bodyline at the complainant Wally Hammond, in such a way as to disfigure, or to mortally injure him.

"You are further charged that on another occasion, even against the advice of your countrymen, you did deliberately attack in a similar manner the Honourable F. S. G. Calthorpe, the captain of the M.C.C. touring team.

"How do you plead?"

Learie argued his own case. It was towards this end that he had studied law. He pleaded extenuating circumstances. He had been provoked. In Wally's case, he had been snubbed. They had got along so well together on the occasion of Learie's first tour of England. At that time Wally Hammond had been practically unknown. Two years later, Wally had hit the headlines. With a 238 not out score in his first big match in the West Indies, he was 'somebody' in cricket. When the boat with the visiting English team had docked in Trinidad, Learie had gone down to meet Wally, but Wally had ignored him. Or so at least it had seemed to Learie. His pride and black dignity had been hurt. Ten years later, the two of them had become friends again, but the record of their differences was still in the Judge's book.

As far as Calthorpe was concerned, had not an England bowler bowled short at the West Indian captain, H. B. G. Austin? Surely he could be forgiven for having been tempted to retaliate!

Learie waited, tense, as the Judge summed up the case.

"Not guilty!"

Learie threw his cap into the air, and raced along on the 'Electric Heels' for which he had become famous. His father and his mother were waiting for him. So, too, was his uncle, Victor Pascall.

Once again there was a burst of trumpets. Then all was quiet. And out of the stillness came a voice, "Well done, Learie Constantine, well done! You have played the game on earth. Let there now be, for you, peace and joy in heaven with those you love."

The angels played sweet music on their harps.

Learie looked up, and there was Norma! He stretched out his arms to greet her.

"I could not get here in time to see the match, but I have come now to be with you always," she said simply.

The gates of heaven opened, and as Learie and Norma passed through, shut softly once more behind them.

3 A cricketing tradition

On the green they watched their sons
Playing till too dark to see,
As their fathers watched them once,
As my father once watched me.

Forefathers Edmund Blunden

Learie Nicholas Constantine, the son of Lebrun and Anna Constantine, was born on the 21st of September, 1901. He was of humble origin. His father was the overseer of a cocoa estate, but he often found it difficult to make ends meet. It cannot, therefore, be said that Learie was born "with a silver spoon in his mouth." Nevertheless, it might not be too far wrong to say that he was born "with a cricket bat in his hand." At the age of three, he could be seen, with bat in hand, walking up and down outside his parents' home in Diego Martin, challenging passers-by to bowl him a ball.

Learie's father was a keen cricketer who had gathered other lovers of the game around him and formed a team. In 1895 he had played for Trinidad against an English team which visited the West Indies under the captaincy of Slade Lucas. He had played cricket in Barbados and in British Guiana, and in 1900 he had been selected to tour England with the first West Indies team.

In 1906, he was once again selected to go to England. Selection was one matter, and this was done on the basis of his cricketing ability. Actually joining the team was another matter, and this was dependent on his financial ability. The team sailed without him.

"Whatever are you doing here, Cons?" asked some people in surprise when they saw him standing in the street some time after the boat had sailed.

'Cons', as he was familiarly called, shrugged his shoulders. "I just could not afford the trip," he said.

But his fans would have none of that. He was too good a cricketer to be left behind. A West Indies' team in England without Cons? No, no, no!

They organised a public subscription immediately, chartered a launch, and Cons was on board before the boat with the rest of the team was out of the Bocas.

Cons justified his fans' belief in him. At Lord's, the most famous of all cricket grounds, he scored the first West Indies' century made in England. And it was the inimitable W. G. Grace who bowled!

By the time that Learie was growing up, the name Constantine was a highly-respected one in the West Indian and international cricketing world.

Learie's uncle, St Croix, his father's brother, was another good cricketer, and Learie often watched the two brothers as they practised in a field near his father's home.

Victor Pascall was his mother's brother, and he, too, was an excellent cricketer. He was noted for his slow left-hand bowling. It was Learie's father who had brought Victor's talent to the attention of the Port of Spain cricketing authorities. This led to his being selected, along with Lebrun Constantine himself, to play for Trinidad in the intercolonial tournament against Barbados in 1905.

Before Trinidad, Barbados and British Guiana became independent in the 1960s, they were colonies of Britain. Trinidad and Barbados are islands in the

West Indies. British Guiana (now a republic known as Guyana since independence) is in South America, but it has always been associated with the West Indies.

From as far back as 1865, British Guiana had taken a team to Barbados to play a cricket match. Barbados in turn took a team to British Guiana a few months later. For the next twenty-five odd years, intercolonial matches were played from time to time. By 1893 regular tournaments had been established, with Barbados, British Guiana and Trinidad taking part. At first these matches were played every two years; then they became annual fixtures to which the colonies looked forward keenly. It was an honour to carry off the Cup which was awarded to the winner.

When Learie was about six years old, his father, who was then living on an estate at St Ann's, one day brought home a piece of matting which he had purchased at a bargain price in town. What Thomas Lord had done in England with turf a century before, Lebrun Constantine now did at St Ann's with that piece of matting. He laid his own pitch.

The entire family had a hand in the laying of it. First they rolled hard a wicket of yellow clay, then they stretched the matting tight over the clay and nailed it down. The 'Constantine Pitch' became the training ground of many budding cricketers, including Learie, with Lebrun Constantine himself as coach.

Learie's father had his own particular views about coaching. He did not interfere with the youngsters' batting style, but he taught them how to bowl the various types of ball. He bowled at them and they learned to bat. On that home-made pitch, he bowled at them just as he would have bowled at any intercolonial cricketer on any famous pitch.

Playing cricket was fun for Learie and his friends,

but learning to field under his father's guidance was a serious business. No one was allowed to miss a ball and get away without censure or a rap on the head.

"Pay attention!" was his father's favourite injunction. If you paid attention, you did not miss.

Years later, Learie was to attribute his own excellence in the field to those early days under his father's coaching when he either "paid attention" or got a mighty rap on the head.

When he was only a third-standard boy at the government elementary school at St Ann's, Learie was thrilled to have the opportunity to play cricket with the bigger sixth and seventh-standard boys. Even at that age, he believed in the well-known saying, "All good things come to those who wait" – (with the popular addition, "*if you know where to wait.*") And *he* knew where to wait. Right where the bigger boys were playing. His chance came one day, as he had hoped it would. They asked him to fill the gap when one of their colleagues did not turn up to play. They had seen him field before, and they knew that he was good. In the game that followed, Learie excelled himself, as if to justify their having chosen him. 47 not out was his score.

If, however, he thought that this performance would have helped him to get into other matches with the bigger boys, Learie was mistaken. Practise with them subsequently? Certainly. He was good enough for that. But play in matches? No! After all, he was only a *third*-standard boy!

At the St Ann's Roman Catholic school to which he was transferred when he was about twelve years old, Learie came under the influence of the head teacher, Mr Andrew de Four, who took a keen interest in cricket, and saw to it that the boys who liked the game practised regularly. By the time he was fourteen, Learie was captain of the First XI. Bearing the name Constantine was not exactly a hindrance to Learie where cricket was concerned.

When he became a young man, Learie's entry into first-class cricket, playing for Victoria, followed only three games played in the Second XI. In the third game he had hit out hard as his father had always insisted he should, and he had scored 50 runs out of the 72 made by his side prior to the game having been stopped by rain.

In spite of the fact that his father, who was captain of Victoria's First XI, did not like having him play first-class cricket at too early an age, there was nothing now to hold Learie back. Constantine senior knew the dangers that could assail a young man pitchforked into playing with men who were far more experienced than he. His spirit could be broken, and his whole cricketing future damaged. Lebrun did not want that to happen to his son Learie, but there was nothing much that could be done about it now, except to give him as much good advice as possible.

It was Uncle Victor, who was already well-known for his slow left-hand bowling, who practised a lot with Learie at the nets. And Learie quickly learned everything that Uncle Victor could teach him of the many tricks that bowlers used. They formed a useful pair in a match, one bowling, the other taking the catches that were almost inevitable. Learie became a wizard at fielding, and the crowds enjoyed watching him.

"Like father, like son," they said. If, after a while, the son began to outshine the father, this seemed only natural. Just how much the older man was prepared to sacrifice in order to give the younger one the opportunity to get into the limelight was not generally known.

After getting into an adult club First XI team, the next step on the ladder of success for a young cricketer in the West Indies is to get into his Island XI. Learie succeeded in doing this after only one season. His father did not compete in the trial games from which selections were made for the Trinidad XI which would play in the next intercolonial tournament against British Guiana. At the time, Learie had no idea that his father had deliberately pleaded "pressure of work" in order to ensure that if only one Constantine was chosen (as one almost inevitably would be) that that one would be Learie.

Learie's debut in intercolonial cricket does not make particularly thrilling reading. Because of a misunderstanding about the time at which the match would begin, he turned up late for the very first game played against British Guiana. His subsequent interview with the captain, Major Harragin, did not contribute to his happiness. Nevertheless, he was selected for the following match which was played against Barbados. He got there in time all right, but so far as adding to the score was concerned, he might just as well not have been there.

A brilliant catch when his side took the field compensated in part for the 0 of his first innings. Challenor and Tarilton, outstanding Barbadian batsmen, were at the wickets. Victor Pascall was bowling. Learie had practised with his uncle long enough as to know just what to expect from each ball Pascall sent down. Fielding at second slip, he saw both Challenor and Tarilton cross the first hurdle. Then Pascall came down again. At one moment, the ball was in contact with the edge of Tarilton's bat; the next moment it was in the hand of Learie who had anticipated what would happen. The resulting cheer from the stands warmed his heart.

Next day, with Challenor batting, Pascall again provided the opportunity for Learie to make a brilliant catch. Again the crowd was ready to warm his heart with their cheers as the ball reached his hand. Up in the air he threw it as he caught it, and down again it came, this time to the ground. A chill spread over all, as Learie learned a lesson.

Trinidad had won the first match against B.G., but rain put a stop to the one against Barbados who retained the Cup. Regardless of who ended up with the Cup, the papers raved about the performance of the Trinidadians Pascall, St Hill and Wiles. C. L. R. James wrote some verses paying tribute to Pascall. The great and famous men all came. "But – " said James, "Pascall bowled."

In 1922, Learie, his father, and his uncle, Victor Pascall, were members of the Trinidad team that played in the tournament against British Guiana. His father had been asked at the last minute to play because Rogers, the regular cover point, had been dropped from the side.

Learie was asked to play at cover, a new experience for him, but by the end of the game, his father, his uncle, and the captain had nothing but praise for him. He himself was pleased. He knew that there was still a lot for him to learn about his new position on the field, but he enjoyed the thrill of knowing that he had not let his side down. More important still, perhaps, was the knowledge that he had not proved unworthy of the name he bore.

4 England, here I come

Oh, to be in England now that April's there,
And whoever wakes in England sees, some morning, unaware,
That the lowest boughs and the brushwood sheaf
Round the elm-tree bole are in tiny leaf,
While the chaffinch sings on the orchard bough
In England – now!

Home-thoughts from Abroad Browning

Unlike the poet Browning, Learie had as yet no nostalgic feelings for England. It was still for him a foreign country. He felt, however, that it would be veritable heaven on earth were he to be selected to go there to play cricket. For him that would be the next step on the ladder of success.

On the 12th of April, 1923, he was aboard the SS *Intaba* sailing for England. He was healthy and in good spirits. His 'cup of joy' was full.

His performance in three first-class matches had earned for him a place on the West Indies team. Other members of the team were H. B. G. Austin, George Challenor, Percy Tarilton, H. W. Ince and George Francis from Barbados; George Dewhurst, George John, Joe Small and Victor Pascall from Trinidad; C. R. Browne, C. V. Hunter and Maurice Fernandes from British Guiana. The Jamaicans, R. K. Nunes, J. K. Holt, and R. S. Phillips did not travel with the rest of the team.

To Learie, the ocean voyage itself was a source of sheer delight. He observed that "people who write cricket books never say anything about the delights of ocean travel.'' But the cold which greeted them on arrival was something of a shock to the newcomers to a temperate country. The season was well on its way before many of them ceased to shiver and suffer from chill.

Young Constantine

There was no red carpet of welcome laid down for the visiting West Indians; no official plans were made for entertaining them. Except in the case of Austin and Challenor who had visited England before, everything was new and strange to the team. Their desire to see as much of England as they could during their first two weeks' stay there was controlled chiefly by two factors – finance and fear of the cold. There was not much that men could do on thirty shillings per week pocket-money, which was all they had besides their hotel and travelling expenses. And the thirty shillings was often barely enough for the tips they had to give. Is it any wonder then that bed and blankets served as their major attraction outside of breakfast, cricket and tea?

As far as the winning of matches was concerned, the tour began badly for West Indies. With the exception of George Francis, the men for a while could not find their form. For Francis, this tour was the first experience of big cricket, but he emerged from it with the reputation of being a great bowler. Prior to his selection on the team, Francis had been engaged as practice bowler at the Kensington Oval, Barbados. He was not chosen to play in the first match of the tour, but he bowled in the second match played against Sussex, taking 4 for 50 and 6 for 33. On another occasion he took 5 for 27, and against Middlesex 6 for 34. And all this with the quiet air of one not conscious of the magnitude of his achievement.

Learie, meanwhile, had as yet done nothing to distinguish himself in the eyes of England. A duck in his first innings against Hampshire brought banter from Kennedy who had bowled him with a slow ball. But Learie was watching the more experienced English players and learning everything that he possibly could.

The turning point was on its way. With six of their men taken by Francis for 34 in the Middlesex match, Patsy Hendren and Hill were settling down. The score reached 330, with Patsy nearing his second century, while Hill was in the sixties. Learie had bowled only four overs so far. At that stage, both he and George John were raring to have a go at these batsmen who seemed determined not to get out.

The West Indies captain, Nunes, kept Pascall and Francis on the ball, even though neither of them was any longer being effective. It was almost time for the drawing of stumps. Dewhurst, behind the wicket, could take it no longer. The thought of having to come back the following Monday to see Hendren and Hill continue their batting went against the grain.

"Put George John and Constantine on the ball," he begged the captain.

Learie was put on. It was not for nothing that he had been observing Hill all the while. Learie was confident that he could get him out. In the first over, Hill's innings came to an end.

It was John's turn to see what he could do. His first ball hit Patsy Hendren hard on the knee. Hendren rested for a while but, nothing daunted, he came back to play the same stroke. The result was the same. Another blow on the knee again. With John's next ball, Patsy Hendren was dismissed.

Learie bowled a maiden over. He felt that the destinies of the remaining three batsmen were in his hands. He knew just what he would do.

But it was John's over now. As he took his place at cover, Learie pleaded with John to leave some of the tail-enders for him.

"Nothing doing," laughed John. "I want them all for myself."

After about five balls from John, there were no more batsmen left for Learie. John had skittled each for 0.

There was rejoicing among the West Indies' team. The match had been lost, it is true, but only by 70 runs, and they had succeeded in giving English cricketers an insight into the ability of West Indies to hold their own against some of the best strokes the home team had to offer.

The match at Oxford brought Joe Small into the limelight. Small, a Trinidadian, played for Stingo, the great rivals of Learie's club Victoria (or Shannon, as it was later called). According to Learie in *Cricket and I*, Stingo "had a team of bowlers which would make Middlesex or Surrey tremble today," and Joe was one of them. He was, in fact, an all-rounder. He bowled fast-medium, and had once taken 7 for 77 against an English touring side. He was also a safe catcher. His greatest reputation, however, perhaps lay in the fact that "he hit the ball hard."

Now in this match at Oxford, it was Joe Small who put a stop to the fun which some Oxford undergraduates were having at the expense of the West Indies. Oxford, who had batted first, had scored heavily. Then the West Indies, going in, had started off badly. The undergraduates scoffed. They felt that they had wasted their time in coming to watch the West Indies play.

"The fellows cannot even bat," they thought.

Then Joe Small went to the wicket. He was the first black man on the team to go in.

"Looks powerful," said the undergraduates.

"Let us hope he will do better than the others," shrugged one.

Learie and some of his companions talked to the

Oxford men as they sat in the pavilion.

When asked if Joe Small could hit hard, Learie replied, "Hit hard? There is no one in the University who can hit half as hard as Small."

Joe did not let Learie down. Although he got out after having made only 29, during the course of building up that score he had slammed the ball through the covers so hard that the undergraduates began to take new interest in the game. They were convinced that he must be the hardest hitter the visitors had on their team.

Learie and his friends scoffed at the idea.

"Wait until you see Holt," they said, pointing to a big, black Jamaican. "He can hit even harder than Small."

This was asking too much of the undergraduates to believe. Or was it? Because, perhaps for the first time for the season, Holt batted that day as he had been accustomed to batting back in his native land. Before an hour had passed, he had scored 52, including eleven fours. Straight through the covers he had driven three of his splendid strokes. The Oxonians felt that Holt's performance had clinched the matter of West Indies' hard hitting. No other member of the team could outdo Holt.

"Not so," countered Learie's companions. They pointed to him.

"This one," they continued, "can hit harder than Small and Holt put together."

Even from his younger days, Learie had often been likened to a blacksmith, so powerful were his strokes. At Oxford that day, when he went into the wicket after Holt was out, his anvil rang out loud and clear. No one could deny that he really hit harder than the two who had gone before. 77 in sixty-five minutes, with one six and eleven fours helping to make up his score! And the originality and variety of his shots left the bowlers all amazed.

As for the Oxford undergraduates, they were enthralled by Learie's performance. West Indies now held them in their sway. Like Goldsmith's villagers, those "who came to scoff remained to pray."

The rest of the tour found West Indies gaining the admiration of England more and more. At Lancashire, Joe Small and Maurice Fernandes scored 131 against mighty bowlers like Cecil Parkin, Dick Tyldesley and others of that calibre. In less than two hours Small hit 94, including twelve fours. It was an innings never to be forgotten by the goodly folk of Lancashire. Parkin bowled, and Small lathered him. Cuts, drives, and leg-glances! Joe played them all.

Parkin stated subsequently that Small had played his bowling better than it had been played that season by any English batsman. This, coming from a distinctly clever Lancashire bowler, was indeed a great tribute to a member of the West Indies' team.

Winning matches or drawing them in their own favour now became the customary thing for West Indies. They had found their form. At the Oval the team played against Surrey. In this match, George Francis and C. R. Browne were the outstanding bowlers, getting England all out for 87 before tea. The critics raved about the batting performance of the Barbadian George Challenor who made 155 not out.

"Challenor is one of the best batsmen playing cricket today," stated *The Cricketer*.

But it was not only the bowling and batting of the West Indies' team that impressed England. Their fielding also crippled their opponents. Learie, from his position at cover, retrieved a ball played by Shepherd who had anticipated a normally safe run. But that was the end of Shepherd's innings!

"Magnificent, but not cricket!" observed someone in the pavilion who had never before seen such perfect fielding.

The last match of the tour was played at Scarborough against an XI, handpicked by Mr H. D. G. Leveson-Gower. Hobbs, Tyldesley, Stevens, Douglas, Mann, Fender, Rhodes, Gilligan, Chapman, Parkin and Leveson-Gower himself! One glance at the list would have warned West Indies what they were up against. But which of them would have cared, anyway?

The match turned out to be one of the most interesting ones of the tour. The West Indies' bowlers John, Francis and Browne each had a special interest in the game – to get his 100 wickets! John already had 93, Francis 93, and Browne 96. Each hoped to complete his record.

West Indies went in first, but the wicket was against them. They scored only 110. They had hopes, however, that the same pitch which had been their downfall would be the downfall of Leveson-Gower's men. And well it might have been, had it not been chiefly for Hobbs in their first innings, and a white-coated man in their second.

Hobbs and Stevens opened the batting and the latter's middle wicket was out of the ground by the time he had scored only 1. Bowler Francis was one mark nearer his goal.

Hobbs, who had made only five centuries that season as against Patsy Hendren's thirteen, settled down to bat with ease. Fast balls from John, in-swingers from Browne, they were all the same to him.

Learie Constantine exhibiting full-blooded driving power at the nets

He was caught out by Austin at short-leg off Francis when 38, but he had taken the edge off the West Indies' bowling, and helped his side to score a little over 200. Learie was fascinated by the ease with which Hobbs had played.

West Indies' second innings was no more impressive than their first had been, and they left the other side only 31 runs to make to win the match. Francis by this time had captured 98 wickets, and so had John. Browne still had 96.

Stevens and Hobbs opened once more. It should not take them long to make the required 31 runs. But while his score was 1, Hobbs hit a ball from Francis right into Austin's hands. That was the end of Hobbs! Oh no, it wasn't. Austin dropped the ball. Francis felt that he just had to have his ninety-ninth wicket soon. Then there would be just one more to follow. He bowled again, and Hobbs was out, this time l.b.w. Stevens went at 8, George John taking an impossible sideways catch from his bat. Francis had got his 100 wickets.

It was John's turn now to get the two he needed. Tyldesley reluctantly gave him one, and Rhodes who came in next decided to hold the fort at all costs. John would have none of that. Hell's devils were let loose, and a demon ball hit Rhodes on the pads.

George John was overjoyed.

"How's that?" he shouted gleefully, and the field took up the echo of his shout.

At that stage of the game, the white-coated man was not on West Indies' side.

"Not out," he said.

No score from Rhodes. He faced Francis from the other end. The same tactics from the batsman, and this other bowler got him on the pads! The umpire shook his head again.

"Not out!"

Rhodes soon went for a duck, and Chapman came in. He beat Learie at cover and scored 2 before John shattered his stumps. John had collected his 100 wickets.

Leveson-Gower's men now had 12 runs to get, with 5 wickets still intact. The rest of the match was touch-and-go. The West Indies did not consider winning an impossibility, because their bowlers had been in similar positions before, and had emerged victorious. Why not now?

Mann was facing John who bowled a full pitch. Learie, fielding at cover, knew what it would be like to attempt to stop the ball which came off Mann's bat. The alternative would be to let it go to the boundary. His hand went out, stopped the ball, and in a flash it was in the wicket-keeper's hand. No run off that! That Learie's hand would be swollen for months after was not important then.

Mann was soon caught and Fender joined Douglas. Fender put his pads where his bat should have gone, but for the third time, West Indies' appeal for l.b.w. was in vain. If only that extra man had not been in the game against them, West Indies might yet have won!

The score crept up to 28. A no-ball from John gave three more runs to even up the score, and then Fender got a four to win the match for his side.

West Indies had played against a good Eleven and an umpire, and had lost the match by four wickets, but they had every reason to be proud of their performance. They felt that the team had put West Indies on a firm footing in the cricketing world, and the welcome which they received when they returned home proved that others felt so too.

5 From dusty deeds to sunny fields

Give to me the life I love,
Let the lave go by me . . .

The Vagabond R. L. Stevenson

"When I am an old man sitting by the fireside, I shall warm my hands at that summer."

That was the summer of 1928 when West Indies again toured England. In one particular match during that tour, Learie covered himself with glory, and thereby earned for himself an invitation from Nelson Cricket Club in Lancashire to turn professional.

To Constantine, then twenty-six years of age, this was an offer not to be ignored. In the West Indies at that time, playing cricket did not pay, and playing cricket for a living was the thing that Learie felt he would enjoy doing best of all.

There was a time when he had thought that the law would be his calling in life. The choice of professions open to the coloured boy in his day was limited, but Learie visualised himself in wig and gown. The shortest way to achieve his ambition to become a lawyer would have been for him to go to England to study. Going to England, however, meant spending money which he did not have, so to obtain his goal he chose the long way instead. He became a solicitor's clerk. In Trinidad, if you served as a solicitor's clerk for ten years, you could then take the solicitor's examinations, and this seemed to be the solution to Learie's problem.

For a whole year he concentrated on his job and did not play cricket regularly. But this was irksome to him. Whenever he could get into a chance game, he seized the opportunity to do so. His father gave him no encouragement.

"Make a man of yourself first," was his father's constant advice. And making a man of himself meant sticking to the job.

Eight years of this was enough for Learie. He quit his job as a solicitor's clerk because it did not give him enough time for cricket.

Next he tried the Civil Service, becoming a clerk to the Registrar of Courts. An acting post in the Education Office followed, but again there was the problem of getting leave to play cricket when he wished to do so. H. B. G. Austin, captain of the West Indies team, wanted him to play against M.C.C. in British Guiana in 1926. The Trinidad officials said it was not possible for him to get the necessary leave. H. B. G. Austin, whose father was a Bishop of the West Indies, was himself Senior Member for Bridgetown in the Barbados House of Representatives. He refused to take "No" for an answer. He wanted Constantine to play. He took the matter in hand himself, and Constantine was given leave to play *with full pay*. That something was wrong with the state of cricket in Trinidad was evident.

Between the West Indies' 1923 tour of England and their next one in 1928, three intercolonial tournaments were played and an England team visited the West Indies. It was cricket, cricket everywhere in the Caribbean islands. After the team's performance in England, everyone was enthusiastic about the game, and with the England team expected towards the end of 1925, excitement ran high.

In 1924, Barbados was the scene of the first of the three tournaments. The next was played in Trinidad, with the home team emerging winners of the Cup. In September 1925, British Guiana hosted the next tournament. Barbados and B.G. had to play first, and then the winner would meet Trinidad.

Barbados was no match for B.G., so the final struggle was between the latter and Trinidad. It was a ding-dong battle, with every man doing his very best, since selection for the team against the M.C.C. would in the main be based on the players' performances in this tournament.

Faced with the task of making 182 to win the final innings on a fairly poor wicket, Trinidad had scored 162 when Constantine, as ninth man, came in to partner Victor Pascall. Could they hold out for 21 runs? This was a situation that called for care, so they were careful, and together they succeeded in making 15 of the runs. Trinidad retained the Cup, with Ben Sealey helping Learie to wipe off the rest.

The M.C.C. arrived in Barbados in December. Much to his disappointment, Learie was not selected to play in the Tests there. What perhaps hurt most of all was the fact that previously he had received a letter from the Barbados Cricket Committee asking him whether he would be able to play against the M.C.C. if he were selected.

Victor Pascall, George John, Dewhurst, Small and St Hill had each received a similar letter and, needless to say, each had gladly said that he would be available. Of the six, however, he had been the only one not selected when the time came, and he could not understand the reason for the omission. Contrary to the rumour in circulation, he knew that he was in good physical condition, but he had to be satisfied with hearing about the Test.

With the Hon. F. S. G. Calthorpe as captain, the M.C.C. side comprised the Hon. L. H. Tennyson, Percy Holmes, Hammond, Captain Jameson, Bennett, Watson, Kilner, Crawley, Dales, Root, Collins and Smith – a good side for any team to meet. Still with the memory of the success of the 1923 tour fresh in mind, West Indies had no fear of such a team or any other that Calthorpe might have brought.

M.C.C. lost their match against Barbados by an innings. The Test against the West Indies followed, but rain put an end to each of the two games played there.

Learie was selected to play in Trinidad. Both matches between M.C.C. and the Island Team were drawn. Then M.C.C. won the Test match by five wickets, but the West Indies had given a good account of themselves. Bowling at one stage to Holmes, Learie, in his inimitable style, followed the ball down the pitch, and as Holmes played a defensive stroke somewhat too quickly, Learie stretched out his hand and caught the ball while he was about three feet away from the batsman.

Learie went with the West Indies team for the Test in British Guiana. There again rain prevented a decisive end to the game, but not before Challenor and Dewhurst, and then C. R. Browne, among others, had shown M.C.C. in a positive manner that the West Indies could hold their own against the best in the game. Again Learie had the opportunity to dismiss Holmes who was batting as if he had no intentions of getting out. West Indies, opening the game, had scored 462, and M.C.C. with a first innings' total of only 264 had had to follow on. When they eventually passed West Indies' score by 45, they had only two more wickets to fall. It was at that stage that the rain gods showered their blessings on M.C.C.

Before returning home, M.C.C. went on to Jamaica where they played three matches, winning one and

Learie holding the Lancashire League Championship Cup

drawing two. Learie and the others did not go to Jamaica.

February 1927 and the intercolonial tournament held in Barbados – a tournament which Learie could never have forgotten, no matter how long he might have lived.

Then came 1928, and forthcoming was the English tour that changed his life. With it came, too, a promise to Learie from Trinidad Leaseholds that if he were selected to join the team his job would be waiting for him when he returned from England. It was H. B. G. Austin who brought Learie the news that he had been selected. What more could a young man ask of life? The opportunity to play cricket in England once more!

Derbyshire, Essex, then Surrey, with Learie enjoying every moment of each game! At Derbyshire, with his side batting in the last innings and needing 40 more to win with 2 wickets in hand, he goes in. From his bat flash five fours and a three, and then eight in another over. The runs are made, and the match is won, and with the winning of that first match, a feeling of exhilaration pervades the team. Nothing could go wrong after that.

A century for Learie at Essex, 94 scored in an hour, three sixes and fourteen fours. For him, 1928 was a great year. A torn muscle as a result of the Surrey match did not deter him from playing in the Middlesex one that followed later – the Middlesex match which led to the newspapers giving him so much publicity. "Constantine beats Middlesex single-handed," they said, and Nelson Cricket Club in Lancashire invited him to join them as professional.

In 1929 Learie went to Nelson, there to begin a life that was new and strange.

6 Nelson takes Learie to her heart

"From quiet homes and first beginning,
Out to the undiscovered ends,
There's nothing worth the wear of winning,
But laughter and the love of friends."

Dedicatory Ode Hilaire Belloc

"Ee, Mister, asta bin down t'pit?"

The little boy with the broad Lancashire accent stopped suddenly, and stared at Learie in wide-eyed astonishment. He had never before seen a coloured man.

Learie, walking down the road to purchase a newspaper on his second Sunday morning in Nelson, gave a half-smile. He would have to get accustomed to such stares, and to the newness of Nelson generally.

He was happy to get away from the stuffiness of office life in Trinidad, and into the freshness of the open air, where he could concentrate on playing the game that meant so much to him. But he had no idea how he would fit into the unaccustomed pattern. Playing cricket as an amateur was one thing. You batted, bowled and fielded for the sheer joy of playing cricket. If you made a century one day, and a duck another, it did not really matter. No Empire was lost thereby. Playing as a professional, however, was something quite different. Much of the game depended on you.

It was the job of the professional to help his side as much as possible. He had to protect the young amateurs of his team by arranging to bear the brunt of the attack of the professional on the other side. He had to encourage his men, and give them confidence. He had to make plenty of runs, to play bright cricket, to win matches, and most of all, to draw the crowds, for, to the clubs, crowds meant money.

In League matches, whenever a batsman made 50 runs, a collection for him was immediately taken up. The spectators dug into their pockets and paid willingly on such occasions. Anything to encourage a bright game! Learie himself became the recipient of such generosity on many an occasion.

Life in Nelson was, in many ways, an unforgettable experience for him. He found League cricket fascinating. The Lancashire folk take a very keen interest in cricket. The League grounds are good, and Saturday matches which are played from 2 p.m. until 7 p.m. draw thousands and thousands of the population in each area.

Burnley, Nelson, Colne, Bacup, Todmorden, East Lancashire, Enfield, Church Haslingden, Ramsbottom, Lowerhouse, Accrington and Rawtenstall were the clubs which comprised the Lancashire League when it was first started. Rishton joined after a short while. After the first year, Todmorden dropped out, but rejoined later. Bury dropped out altogether after having played for two seasons. The cricket fan who has read or heard about these clubs is thrilled when visiting England for the first time to see the familiar names as he passes through the various towns and villages.

Learie found the standard of League cricket played to be very high, and stated that it would be a great mistake for any first-class cricketer to believe that he could "just walk into the League and proceed to be a success." League cricket called for a special technique, and the cricketer who wished to be a success had first of all to learn what that technique was. No bowler's reputation was sacred to a Lancashire League batsman. It was knocked about with the same ease that a ball from the hand of a 'nobody' was knocked about.

In 1919 Alderman H. Worsley had presented a cup to the Lancashire League, and the competition for this cup, known as the Worsley Cup, has been one of the interesting features of League matches since then.

Throughout the years, it is the professional cricketer who has helped to make League cricket what it is. In Learie's day, Nelson was one of the foremost clubs in the League. Even today it still holds an honoured place. The inhabitants of the town are keen cricket fans who give unstinted support to the game. The club has always tried to obtain the services of a good professional. Prior to the appointment of Learie, first McDonald from Australia, and then Blanckenberg from South Africa, had been the professionals at Nelson.

From a cricketing point of view, Learie's first season at Nelson was little short of wonderful for him. He made the occasional century, got an average of 34, and his total number of runs was just under 1,000. In bowling, he took 88 wickets in 361 overs, for an average of 12. Even though in subsequent seasons his figures were more impressive, no season brought him greater satisfaction or joy than did his first at Nelson. He had no regrets about having given up his job as a solicitor's clerk.

"It was a splendid summer and the memory of it is golden," he wrote in *Cricket in the Sun*, "How I should have hated to be a lawyer with not one golden summer in my life!"

As summer drew to an end, Learie was asked to take his team to Scotland for a week of cricket against the various counties. It was an enjoyable week. The team played well, Learie himself scoring 175 not out on one occasion. Sightseeing tours organised by their host added to the team's enjoyment.

1930 came, and with it Learie's second season at Nelson! It was in April 1929 that he had first taken up his job with the club. It did not take him long to establish himself in the eyes of all Nelson as a fine cricketer. Those who saw him for the first time in those days talk still of the sensational thrill it was to watch him on the field.

Among those who were struck by the magic of his personality was John Kirk, now a well-known Manchester solicitor. At the time, John was only a boy of nine, but he still remembers the electric atmosphere that was generated whenever Learie appeared. To John and to many others it always seemed that something was about to happen. And they had to watch to see what that something was.

Michael Parkinson was another youngster at the time when Learie first came to Nelson. Except on the films, Michael had never before seen a black man. Going back to the memory of those days, "He generated excitement," said Parkinson, "like a man walking a tightrope without a safety net."

Learie spent nine years as the pro. at Nelson. During those nine years, Nelson won the Championship seven times. Financially, he was a great asset to the club. From an overdraft of $15,000 when Learie joined them, Nelson showed a profit within three years' time. There was no doubt whatever in the minds of anyone that Learie "was worth his weight in gold."

Outside of cricket, however, life for a while was not

very easy for Learie. An oddity in Nelson, so far as colour was concerned, Learie was extremely sensitive. Little boys followed him around just to look at him. A coloured man was a curiosity. They longed to touch the blackness of his skin to see if it would rub off.

It was his wife Norma who helped Learie over the difficult times. When he tended to be fiery, Norma was calm and self-assured. After a time – it seemed to them like a long, long time – they became as much a part of the town which was their adopted home, as the original townsfolk themselves. But it had taken patience and understanding on their part. Learie never ceased to acknowledge his debt to Norma who with her level-headedness had helped him considerably over the difficult spots. And when in later years he was away from Nelson on cricket tours, as often he was, life went on smoothly for the Constantine family.

C. L. R. James, author, lecturer, and a fellow Trinidadian, spent a year in Lancashire as a guest of the Constantines. Learie befriended him in many ways. He collaborated with Learie in the writing of the latter's first book *Cricket and I*. In his own book *Beyond a Boundary*, James describes the effect which Learie had on the people of Lancashire. He states that "Constantine by his cricket, by the demeanour of himself and his wife in what all could realize was no easy situation, by 1932 had created an enormous interest in the West Indies and West Indians."

First Learie, and then 'C. L. R.', while he lived in Lancashire, used to be invited to speak at meetings, and their audiences were always highly appreciative. In those days, Learie, being a professional cricketer, kept out of politics. There was no reason, however, why James should. As a result of these talks, the English began to know more about West Indians and to understand them better.

As the Constantine family 'grew' upon Lancashire, so, too, did Lancashire 'grow' upon them. When at the end of the 1930 season, West Indies sent a team to Australia, Learie was chosen to go with them. He liked the Australians, and left their country with many pleasant memories. Before a cheering crowd he broke Sutcliffe's record of 132 runs before lunch by himself scoring 147. At the end of the last Test, the Australians paid him a great compliment. They asked for his photograph to place in the pavilion at Sydney – a rare honour reserved for only a few players.

When Learie left Australia and returned to Nelson, he felt that he was 'coming home'. Lancashire had conquered him. "Lancashire people are grand folk," he wrote; ". . . if they give their friendship it is wholeheartedly given."

The people of Lancashire had given their friendship to Learie and his family. Whatever reserves Learie might have built up in the early days were gradually broken down. The people of Nelson had grown to like him and to respect him as a person. They even asked him to be Mayor of the town.

Learie and Norma found themselves surrounded by genuine friends to whom colour of skin was of no importance. The Edmundsons, the Prestons, the Lamberts, the Kirks, the Whittles, the Thorntons – these were some of the many families to whom the Constantines had endeared themselves.

Learie's popularity with the working man was immense. The ordinary man in the street believed in him. Whenever he visited the Lambert bat-making works at Lomeshay, work automatically came to a standstill.

Elizabeth Whittle, John Kirk's little niece, was one

of the few persons in Lancashire who was not impressed by Learie in the flesh. Watching him play cricket with the older children on the lawn of her parents' home, her comment was, "He can't really play cricket – not like on the telly!"

When after nine years as professional with the Nelson Cricket Club, Learie decided that it was time for him to be 'marching on', and accepted a job with the Rochdale Club, no one in Nelson wanted to see him go. Learie went to Rochdale, but his home remained at Nelson which had taken him to her heart, and to whom he had given his.

Twenty-five years later, the spell which Learie Constantine had cast on Nelson was still unbroken. On Saturday, 20th April, 1963, Learie was made an Honorary Freeman of the Borough of Nelson. He thus became the sixth Freeman in the seventy-four years since the town was incorporated as a Borough. A signal honour indeed!

Nelson had truly taken Learie to her heart.

7 Memorable matches

> There's a breathless hush in the Close tonight
> Ten to make and the match to win—
> A bumping pitch and a blinding light,
> An hour to play and the last man in.
>
> *Vitai Lampada* Henry Newbolt

Somewhere in every cricketer's *Book of Memories*, there is a section which deals with the matches which he liked best of all. No matter what the reason might be for his fondness for a particular match, to the cricketer it remains unforgettable, and he relives it and is ready to recount it for all who wish to hear.

The match that Learie considered as the greatest one in which he had ever played took place in Barbados in 1927. It was not the West Indies playing against either England or Australia (great as matches with them as opponents might have been), but Trinidad versus Barbados in the final phase of an Intercolonial Tournament with Trinidad, British Guiana and Barbados as the teams.

Trinidad held the Cup, and British Guiana was to play Barbados first, and the winner would play Trinidad. From the outset, however, Trinidad knew that Barbados would be the team it would have to play. It was not easy for anyone to beat a Barbados team on its home grounds, and British Guiana stood little chance of accomplishing that feat.

The M.C.C. had not been able to do it in 1911. On that occasion Barbados had batted only twice, beating them by an innings each time. In 1912 Barbados had scored 520 for 6 and 445 against M.C.C. again. Seven years later, Barbados were still top scorers at home, with 489 and 623 for 5 against Trinidad. In 1924 Jamaica had seen them score 426 for 2 declared. Barbados at home batted with the supreme confidence born of ability and past successes. In words similar to the Psalmist they seemed to say, "The Lord is on our side. Whom then shall we fear?"

But with the Cup in hand, Trinidad was determined that it would not be lightly taken from them, if it was to be taken from them at all. Pascall, Small, André Cipriani, W. St Hill, Wiles, Roach, Ben Sealey, Edwin St Hill and Constantine himself were among those who comprised the Trinidad team.

Undoubtedly it was difficult to beat Barbados in Barbados, particularly since they had such outstanding opening bats as Challenor and Tarilton who so often scored centuries when they played.

Trinidad won the toss on a rainy morning and sent Barbados in to bat. On this occasion, neither Challenor nor Tarilton did his customary scoring. Challenor made 11, Tarilton 0.

Trinidad began their innings with a few brilliant boundaries from André Cipriani, but their lifted spirits were later depressed when W. St Hill was caught before he had made a single run.

Better luck was to follow next day when both Small and Wiles took over the century scoring. As for Wiles, a Barbadian playing for Trinidad, his was a particularly brilliant accomplishment which served a double purpose. Not only did he prove to Trinidadians that he could play as well on turf as he could on matting, but he also showed the Barbadians that as a batsman he could beat the intercolonial record of 180 runs made by the wizard Barbadian batsman Percy Goodman, some twenty years before.

Trinidadians were happy about the performance of their adopted son. The Barbadians were 'getting licks' at home at last. Returning to the dressing-room at the end of the day's play, with his score at 191 not out, Wiles is reported to have said, "Boys, I can die now!" He survived long enough in that match to add one more run to his score before cutting at a wide ball from Griffith and being caught.

Trinidad ended the innings with a total of 559 which put them jubilantly 392 runs ahead of Barbados, and almost assured of victory.

Starting with a deficit of 392 runs is enough to daunt the spirits of any average cricketer. But who ever classified Barbadians as average cricketers?

"Now is the time to show the renegade Wiles and the Trinidadians the sterner stuff of which we are made," the famous opening bats Challenor and Tarilton seemed to say as they walked to the wicket. Barbados walked with them in confidence. Wiles must learn that he could not with impunity take from Barbados the record that was theirs!

Time passed. 223 runs on the scoreboard. The two batsmen were batting still.

"I have bowled at Hobbs and Sutcliffe at the Oval," wrote Constantine, "and against Woodfull and Ponsford at Sydney, but Tarilton and Challenor batting for Barbados at the Kensington Oval were worthy to stand in that great company."

Some time later, Challenor played a ball to cover, and Constantine was there with his hands on the grass to catch the ball.

"Howzzat?" went up, but the umpire said "Not out," and the batting went on steadily. When the score was 292, Tarilton was run out.

All eyes now centred upon Challenor. Would he pass Wiles' score? He did, and the cheering was both loud and long. Barbados had retrieved the honour which earlier had been snatched from them.

389 runs and only two men out, 423 and only 3 men out! Pascall, Edwin St Hill, and Constantine all bowled their best. But the Barbadian batsmen batted still. 4 for 568, 5 for 637, 6 for 646, 7 for 726. And Barbados declared their innings closed.

Trinidad would have to make 342 to win the match. They lost by 125 runs. To Challenor, Tarilton and Hoad, who had headed the Barbados batting list, had been accorded the distinction of scoring a century in each of the innings.

"For them, and indeed for all of us," wrote Constantine, "it was a tournament of tournaments."

Another match that Learie liked was one played against Middlesex in the 1928 West Indies Tour of England.

In a match played at Surrey just before, Learie had torn a muscle, and the doctor had recommended that he should not play against Middlesex. But Learie knew that his team needed him. Until then, they had had a bad tour. Apart from the fast bowlers Griffith, Francis and himself, the team had performed poorly. Financially, they were in a bad way, and Learie knew that unless something could be done in the Middlesex match to kindle the interest of the sporting public, the forthcoming Tests would be a dismal failure. And the West Indies could ill afford the resulting damage which this would mean both to their reputation and their pockets.

Doctor's orders or no doctor's orders, Learie made up his mind that he would play, and play he did. He scored a century in an hour, and his team won by three wickets.

The newspaper headlines ran, "Constantine beat Middlesex single-handed." No wonder that Learie remembered this match!

Sir Pelham Warner, writing in his book *Lord's 1787–1945* described the match as being Constantine's 'with a vengeance'. He thought that by it Learie had covered himself with glory. In the county's second innings had Constantine not taken seven wickets in fourteen overs and three balls for 57 runs – the last six in six overs and three balls for 11 runs?

"Two of his strokes," wrote Sir Pelham, "I shall remember to my dying day. The first was when he hit a good length ball of Allen's over extra-cover's head far up into the Grand Stand, and the second when he played back to Hearne with such tremendous force that the ball, after striking the rails, ricochetted among the seats, scattering the members of the M.C.C. and of Middlesex, and bringing destruction to wood-work and paint. On its ferocious passage from the bat Hearne very pluckily put one of his hands in the way of the ball, and was so badly hurt that he played no more cricket that season!"

It was as a result of that Middlesex match that Learie was approached by Nelson Cricket Club to become a professional. He accepted, and there began a long and pleasant association. It is said that as a result of this offer, Constantine became the highest paid cricketer in the world.

Another memorable match was one which the West Indies played against Australia in 1931. There was West Indies taking advantage of a sticky wicket and sending in their opponents to bat when only 251 runs ahead! What a thrill it would be to see the Australians

Going in to bat at Nelson

fall victim to this ruse, as fall they must, according to West Indian predictions!

But the Australian opening bats, Woodfull and Ponsford, upset their calculations. They settled down and easily scored 50. The sun meanwhile rolled over in the heavens and seemed to smile on Australia. The wicket, no longer sticky, was all 'Down Under' could wish for.

But if the sun had gone over to Australia's side, Learie was still there for the West Indies. Woodfull was caught; Ponsford was caught. Learie was in his element! The great Bradman, bowled by Griffith, was out for a duck; Constantine delivered an off-break to Kippax, and Roach's hands were there to catch him.

The sun looked down and questioned what was going on. Australia looked up and added run to run until the score was 214. All was not lost! Two wickets to fall, and 37 runs to win! Would Australia do it? Learie thought not.

Thrills upon thrills, and Learie catches Grimmett, and Fairfax is run out. West Indies had scored their first Test victory over Australia!

Another thrilling match was in that second Test against England played at Queen's Park Oval, Port of Spain in 1934–35. England had won the first Test played in Barbados, and won it by four wickets after a great sporting game.

The English captain Wyatt considered that he had the best team England had ever sent to the West Indies. Headley, Ellis Achong, Martindale, and Constantine were among those on the West Indies side who made up their minds that England should not have everything their way.

Wyatt won the toss, but sent West Indies in first to bat. Derek Sealy missed his century by 8 runs;

Constantine missed his by 10. What a day that was for him, bat flashing in the sunshine, ball going just where it was meant to go – except just once when it landed in Patsy Hendren's hands.

West Indies all out for 302; England going in, not doing too well at first, then holding on grimly until they had 258!

Forty-four runs was not too big a lead, but it was all that the West Indies needed to send them into the second innings jubilant and determined.

Headley and Sealy gave the crowds the cricket which they had paid to see. The order of the day was double figures for West Indies' batsmen. Then came Skipper Grant's declaration at 280, giving England 325 runs to make in 3½ hours if they were to win!

But England knew soon enough that they could not win. Not with Constantine bowling like an angel at one time, and like a demon at another, and all the while the West Indian crowd yelling and cheering and burning with the desire to see England beaten and the game won!

No, England could not win. But, by golly, they'd have a right royal try for a draw!

Townsend and Farrimond, Paine and Grant, Smith, Hendren and Wyatt out by tea; Ames seeing Hendren go. Then he and Leyland playing for time, while West Indies bowled, bowled and bowled again. "Bodyline!" charged the umpire as Constantine caused Ames to duck. And Learie was taken off.

But the crowd would have none of that!

Then Ames was out, and Iddon was in, and Iddon was out before Ames had reached the pavilion, and England's score was 103 for 9!

Holmes came out. Five minutes to go before the end of play! And the crowds could hear a pin drop.

Constantine had never known such silence before.

But let him describe those last few minutes as he does in *Cricket in the Sun.*

"The ball flashed down in the evening sun, went past the wicket, and Holmes was running a bye. Another bye. Another bye. Yes, they would not hit them – they would not risk anything – they just stole byes quietly, with perfect timing, and waited for the clock to defeat us.

"Four minutes to go. Three minutes. Two minutes. One minute.

"I was bowling the last over. Plan them now, Learie! the straight fast one, the one to leg, the tempting one outside the off stump that looks too tempting and is obviously a trap and is left severely alone by Leyland. Less than half a minute to go, two balls to bowl, and the Test ends – in a draw?

"Up to the wicket just as fast as before, identical action, but just the faintest slur of that bowling hand, a ball just a shade slower but looking exactly the same as the rest. Leyland, playing hesitantly forward, just too late, feels it smack on his pad.

" 'S 'at!"

"You could have heard them in New York or Los Angeles.

"No mistaking it, no doubting it – a clean l.b.w., and the match won with the fifth ball of the over, with sixteen seconds to go. West Indies win by 217 runs.

"Ten thousand people rushed the pitch. We tried to dodge, but it was no good, and I found myself shoulder-high, swaying and bumping amidst yells and laughter, and a rat-tat-tat of blows on the back, head, arms, legs – anywhere anyone could reach. Why not be honest and say I enjoyed it like mad? It was one of the moments when one sipped nectar with the gods."

8 Bodyline and all that

"The time has come," the Walrus said,
"To talk of many things:
Of shoes – and ships – and sealing wax –
Of cabbages – and kings."

Alice Through the Looking-glass Lewis Carroll

That Constantine was a man who, like E. W. Swanton, saw cricket from all angles, is evinced by the fact that he has expressed his views on practically every aspect of the game; and expressed them fearlessly. For the benefit of those who have not had the opportunity and the pleasure of reading his books on cricket, a summary of some of those views is given. Bodyline, slow bowling, practice, coaching, umpiring, barracking – he has written about them all, and more!

Bodyline : mention the word 'bodyline', and immediately into the minds of cricket fans of the 30s there will spring the names Jardine and Larwood – English names notorious in the Australian annals of cricket.

Described by Swanton as a "rancorous tour", the 1932 visit to Australia of an England team under D. R. Jardine engendered more bitterness in the cricketing world than, perhaps, anything else before or since has done. Ordered by Jardine, and carried out by Larwood, bodyline bowling almost led to an abrupt ending of the tour.

What is 'bodyline'? Constantine, in his book *Cricketers' Carnival*, describes it as "bowling which travels along the pitch at upwards of eighty miles an hour (i.e. *very* fast), which is bumped so as to fly over the wicket or in the vicinity of the batsman's face, and which is delivered with a field of seven or eight men on the leg side."

The opponents of bodyline considered that its main purpose was to damage the batsman so that he had to retire hurt, or else "to force him to cover up his face with his bat in such a way that the ball lifts into the hands of the leg-side fielders." They felt that the batsman had no other reply to such bowling.

Learie did not agree with this view at all. He was convinced that no bowler of bodyline ever set out to maim the man, but rather to intimidate him first – to make him aware that the ball can be made to do something – and as a result of that intimidation, then to bowl him out. He showed, too, that covering up his face with his bat in such a way that the ball lifted into the hands of the leg-side fielders was not the only reply the batsman had to such bowling.

Learie showed that even though at the time it was not known as 'bodyline', he himself had used that type of bowling back in 1926 against the England player Wally Hammond. "He was knocking my straight ones about in a very pretty style, so that I shortened one or two on the leg, to see whether he would get out of his wicket. Young Wally did not like them and complained, but Lord Tennyson told him to shut up and bat – which he did very well."

"Do you see why I say bodyline is not dangerous?" asked Learie, and he continued by pointing out that every batsman could try what Tennyson advised, and that would put an end to bodyline for that innings.

He cited also the occasion of his second tour of England with West Indies in 1928 when Larwood was "bumping them down deliberately at us every now and then." What was the result? The batsmen who flinched got out. Those who hit the ball stayed in.

"That," concludes Learie, "is really all there is to it."

To pretend that the danger of fast bowling in the 1930s was something new in cricket is to shut one's eyes to facts. Neville Cardus, writing in *English Cricket* tells us that "the perils faced by batsmen on the crude turf of the older times against fast bowling – and it *was* fast – could not be anticipated; they came without warning; the best length ball might at any moment fly upward and knock a man out."

He continues by repeating the story of the accident to young George Summers at Lord's, as told originally by Richard Daft, the Nottinghamshire classic. "We were playing Notts v. the M.C.C., and Platt was bowling at a terrific pace that season. Summers and Bignall were batting in our second innings, and the former, before he had scored, was struck on the cheek bone by a rising ball from Platt, and was carried off the field insensible. The blow caused concussion of the brain, and the poor fellow died three days afterwards."

"The danger of severe physical hurt has almost passed from first-class cricket," wrote Cardus on the same page. "Even when Larwood bowled the bodyline attack, so called, nobody was killed or critically injured."

Whatever else might be said of bodyline bowling, it would seem that it might be summed up as "fast bowling which the batsman dealt with, if he did not want it to deal with him."

"Men are killed in boxing, polo, baseball, hunting, Association and Rugby football – even fishing," pointed out Learie, but "no one suggests banning these sports or losing any outposts of Empire over it."

Slow bowling: in an essay on Constantine, Neville Cardus, in his book *Good Days*, wrote, "All West Indians who come to the game try to bowl fast as a matter of course; to train a West Indian slow bowler you must begin with his grandfather."

While considering Cardus to be the most beautiful writer of this generation on cricket, and a genius at sizing up the characters and powers and faults of cricketers, Constantine wanted to prove him wrong on this question of the West Indian and slow bowling. He set out deliberately to refute Cardus's statement.

Even at the time when he knew that his bowling equalled some of the fastest the cricket world had ever seen, Learie realised that the time would come when he must slow down. Where batting was concerned he intended to develop in his own way, striving after getting runs; on the field, he wished still to deserve his nickname 'Electric Heels'. It was therefore in the area of bowling that he must conserve his energies in recognition of advancing age. And the desire to refute Cardus's statement added incentive to his decision.

Towards this end, he practised for years in League cricket, and his success as a slow bowler can be measured by his bowling figures in the 1939 West Indies tour when he took 123 wickets for an average of 16·6 runs.

There is no need to start with a cricketer's grandfather to produce a West Indian slow bowler! This was clear. Constantine had proved beyond doubt that even a change from a fast bowler into a slow one could be effected in one man's lifetime.

There were other West Indian slow bowlers of note – Victor Pascall and Ellis Achong (to mention but two) – whose grandfathers had in no way been

involved in their development in the art of slow bowling.

Practice: whether it was in the area of batting, or bowling, or fielding, it was Constantine's belief that good cricket is mostly a matter of constant practice. To support this view, he quoted the cases of several well-known cricketers who attributed their success to practice – a lot of it.

Jack Hobbs is reported to have said that he learned much of his batting "with a lamp-post for a wicket in a Cambridge street." Playing against a brick wall helped the great Australian Don Bradman to learn his timing.

Set the task of counting and packing some 4,000 oranges every morning before leaving for school, Constantine himself learned to bowl by practising against a bamboo stick with all the unripe oranges.

"Practise, practise, practise!" This was what Learie's father had constantly advised him and other young cricketers to do. Now this was what he in turn advised all who wanted to become adept at the game to do.

"Miraculous! Marvellous!" shouted jubilant West Indians as Learie made a slip-catch off Hardinge to Griffith's bowling in Kent in 1928.

Learie smiled. He knew it was no miracle. Before 1927 he had been a good cover-point, but when he decided to be "an out-and-out fast bowler", he knew that slip should be his place. He made up his mind to concentrate on slip-fielding, and he practised sedulously. In a year he was taking with ease slip-catches which would have been impossible before.

On this occasion, he had simply done what he had

Learie showing perfect balance and concentration at speed

done in practice at real or imaginary balls hundreds of times before. And it paid off. The other side had lost a good batsman, and West Indies had saved, only Heaven knows, how many runs.

Practice was what counted in the game.

Coaching: on the subject of coaching, Learie felt that it was easier to "coach all the natural cricket ability out of a player" than "to coach any inspiration into him." Teach basic good style and encourage free development. He maintained that this is what should be done. In 1923, during his first tour of England, he realised the danger of trying to adapt his own natural, unorthodox style to that suggested by his coach. His batting average fell to 9. "Stick to the style that gets you runs," he advised, "and never mind, so long as you achieve that object, what the professors may say about the way you attain it."

Pitches and averages: "If I were President of the M.C.C. (which, pious souls exclaim, Heaven forbid!) I should agitate not only for the excision of the 'dead' class of pitch from the categories of the quick and the dead, but also for the absolute abolition and prohibition of all tables of averages."

Thus wrote Constantine in *Cricketers' Carnival*. And he was not alone in his views on this subject of pitches and averages. In an interview which he granted to Swanton at the end of the 1946–47 Test series in Australia, Don Bradman criticised the existing l.b.w. law which led to "negative, unattractive cricket", and stated that "the laws should be changed to make the game as attractive as possible, not to please the batsmen." Asked then if there were any other ways in which he thought cricket might move with the times, he replied, inter alia, that he thought "that attention must be given to the laws of the game such as the l.b.w. law and the preparation of pitches, so that matches remain a contest of skill rather than endurance."

Neville Cardus also, in the closing paragraphs of *English Cricket* states that not only should the groundsman be ordered to make a fair wicket with as little preparation as is consistent with conditions of local soil rolled to reliability, and not to lifelessness, but also that "the factor of time must be retained in great matches. The players must be up and doing, conscious that they are under a lease of hours . . ."

"But most of all," Cardus continues, "it is the spirit that counts."

On this point, no one could have agreed with Cardus more heartily than Constantine.

"Averages have been the bane of cricket in the past twenty years in England," he observed at the time he wrote *Cricketers' Carnival*. Striving for averages, cricketers were prepared to subject onlookers to the dullest of dull batting. Fun went out of the game.

Learie had never forgotten an occasion in the early days when he played second-class cricket for Victoria. Playing in the second match against Queen's Royal College, he had made 19 not out, of a total score of 68. This had made him very happy indeed, since in the first match he had only scored 6. Full of pride in himself at his performance, he told his father how he had batted for at least an hour for his runs. He waited for the words of approval which he felt would be forthcoming. They never came. "You wasted your time," said his father. "You have a bat in your hand to score runs with, instead of which you stayed there trying not to get out."

Learie was deflated, but he kept in mind his father's

comment.

"Hit the ball! Hit it! Hit it! Let averages take care of themselves!" This is what he must often have said to himself. Certainly, Cardus, the man with an eye for cricket, got the impression that when Learie hit a ball for six he said, "Oh golly, I like it: let me do it again."

Umpiring : "They also serve who only stand and wait." Most people, including writers on cricket, recognise the fact that umpiring is not only a difficult job, but a thankless one as well. It was with Milton's line in mind that Cardus concluded his sympathetic chapter on 'The Umpire', which is found in his book *Good Days.* He considers as worthy of our applause "the men who serve the game by standing – and waiting for the end of the long, long day." And what a long, long day it must seem to those two men whose concentration must never flag from the beginning of the game to its sometimes bitter end – men who have had at times to run for their very lives when their decisions were unpopular with the crowds.

Learie commented unfavourably on the standard of umpiring in Australia. E. W. Swanton, in an article which appeared in 'The Argus' of Melbourne in January 1947, revealed that Australian cricketers themselves were aware that their standard of umpiring was "less admirable than it might be." But the reason for such a situation was not hard to find.

The standard of Test match umpiring in England was high, and owed its superiority to the fact that, usually, Test match umpires had been professional cricketers who knew the game perfectly. Men like Frank Chester and Joe Hardstaff, as Learie pointed out, had to guard their reputations jealously, and so could not afford to make many mistakes.

Because there was less first-class cricket played in Australia than in England, the financial returns to the Australian umpire were necessarily far less than to his English counterpart. Indeed, in terms of money, umpiring in Australia was quite unattractive. Similarly in English League cricket where, in Constantine's day, two umpires between them got £1 from the gate receipts which yielded £75 to the two professional players in the same match! Under such circumstances, who would be eager to serve as an umpire? Learie went so far as to state that seventy per cent of the decisions given in League and Club cricket in England on Saturday afternoons were hopelessly wrong by first-class standards.

Recognition of the cause of the problem, and sympathy in the matter did not in any way close people's eyes to the disastrous effect that bad umpiring had on the game.

"Good umpiring makes good cricket." Learie shared this view with others. No batsman likes to be "umpired out", and the general answer to bad umpiring is dull defensive cricket.

No matter how sincere and unbiased an umpire might be (and Learie was convinced that most Australian umpires were that) he felt that when a fine distinction of judgment had to be made in an instant, errors were inevitable unless the umpire was a man who had had "almost a lifetime of experience of the game."

To close this section on umpiring, a touch of humour might not be out of place, and what better than to repeat a story as told by the master of cricket writers himself – Neville Cardus.

"Once upon a time a cricket match was about to be played between two village clubs of long and vehement rivalry. An hour before the pitching of stumps a visitor to the district walked on to the ground and inspected the wicket. He was greeted by an old man, a very old man. The visitor asked for information about the impending battle, and the ancient monument told him.

"Is your team strong in bowling?" asked the visitor.

"Ay, sir, not so bad," was the answer.

"And who gets most of your wickets?" asked the visitor.

"Why, sir, Oi do," was the reply.

"Heavens," said the visitor, "surely you don't bowl at your time of life?"

"No, sir, Oi be the umpire."

Barracking: "No one could really imagine barracking from the austere precincts of Lord's or the Oval – or Old Trafford!"

How Learie must have turned in his grave during the recent West Indies tour of England. For the "austere precincts" of Lord's which he had written about became one of the ugliest scenes of barracking witnessed on a cricket ground for a long, long time; on this occasion with Boycott as its butt.

Ugly as it might have seemed to many others, hooting and jeering at cricket players was a thing that Learie could conceive of as taking place anywhere else but on those grounds he mentioned above. He thought that it was the sun that made barrackers, and that without them something was lost. He, himself, rather liked them, and never saw any harm in barracking even when it was directed against himself.

How unlike the Australian cricketer, Warwick Armstrong, captain of the team which toured England in 1921! Neville Cardus, in his essay *Cricket Fields and Cricketers*, tells us that Armstrong sat on the grass at

Old Trafford and refused to go on with the game until the crowd, which was in a bad temper, for a wonder, stopped "barracking" him. Ironical this, seeing that Australian crowds were themselves notable barrackers!

After the "bodyline furore" of 1932–33, the M.C.C.'s visit to Australia in 1936 was of major importance. The future of Test cricket between England and Australia probably depended on that tour.

"No barracking" was the rule of the day, and under their excellent captain Allen, the team met a friendly atmosphere wherever they went. It rained a lot during the course of that tour.

Learie might not have been there to witness it, but if, as he said, it was the sun that made barrackers, it was with a vengeance that the sun shone down at Lord's in the summer of 1973.

9 Niggers at the back

'Once riding in old Baltimore
 Heart-filled, head-filled with glee,
I saw a Baltimorean
 Keep looking straight at me.

Now I was eight and very small,
 And he was no whit bigger,
And so I smiled, but he poked out
 His tongue, and called me 'Nigger'.

I saw the whole of Baltimore
 From May until December,
Of all the things that happened there
 That's all that I remember.'

Incident Countee Cullenn

Somewhere between Constantine's two books *Cricket and I* (1933) and *Colour Bar* (1954), the Roman Catholic Church lost forever one of its hitherto devoted sons.

"I am a Roman Catholic," stated Learie in that first book, in all earnestness and sincerity, "so somewhere about the age of twelve I left the St Ann's Government School and went to the St Ann's Roman Catholic School, so that I could be prepared for my first communion."

We can imagine young Constantine having made his first communion – a major event in the life of every Catholic – going about his daily business of school, work and play from Monday until Friday, and then regularly on Saturday afternoons going to Confession, preparatory to taking Holy Communion at Mass on Sunday morning. This was a ritual no good Catholic ever missed.

By the time of *Colour Bar*, however, twenty-odd years later, he had suffered disillusionment, a disillusionment from which he never recovered, and all because of the painful experiences of colour segregation it was his lot to have.

He felt that in cricket or in business one might be prepared to face such things, but "when kneeling and praying, one's armour is off and the hurt seems to enter one's soul."

No longer does he say, with the previously retained fervour of his early youth, "I am a Roman Catholic." Instead, we read, "I *used* to be a Roman Catholic." His devotion is now a thing of the past. But he continues to assert that his belief in God and in the perfect love of Jesus has never wavered, although he has ceased to practise his religion formally.

"I do not make confession or attend Mass any more," he writes, "and if I felt I were dying, I do not think I should send for a priest to give me absolution; I would take my chance of God's forgiveness. This is a dreadful thing for a sincere Roman Catholic to say, but I say it because I have suffered so much, and seen my coloured friends suffer so much, at white priests' and white Roman Catholic worshippers' hands."

On occasion, he was debarred from eating in a London restaurant; he was refused rooms in a London hotel. The memory of these incidents must have rankled. His hurt must have been intense when, at a cricket gathering, as his wife approached a group of white spectators he overheard one woman remark aloud to another, "I see they've let the jungle in upon us."

Perhaps his religious fervour was strong enough then as to allow him to say to himself, "Father, forgive them for they know not what they do." But the incident which served to break his connection with the Church was one which took place in a New York Roman Catholic Church. As he knelt praying, he was rudely told, "Git out o' there! Niggers at the back!"

This was the last straw! Learie got out, never in life to return to that or any other Roman Catholic Church. His soul had been seared.

How different was Learie's reaction from that of a Negro acolyte faced with a situation where his colour was a drawback.

This Negro helped to serve at the altar of a Roman Catholic Church in England. A priest informed him that in future only young persons would be used as acolytes, so there was no further need of his services. However, he would be expected to attend church as a member of the congregation.

The following Sunday, the Negro was there in Church, even though not in his usual place, serving at the altar. But there, serving as usual, were the white-skinned acolytes.

What surprised Learie was the fact that the Negro continued to attend church as though nothing had happened. When Learie angrily remonstrated with him, the Negro calmly replied, "One man has done me a wrong, but that is not going to separate me from God or keep me away from Church."

Years after, when tempted to hit back when hurt by white people, Learie would remember this Negro whose Christian attitude prompted the turning of the other cheek. Dark cheek to turn while white hand strikes? For Learie, this was "the most unkindest cut of all." It was difficult for him to be a true Christian where the turning of the other cheek was concerned; but he knew that the Negro acolyte was right.

It was with a certain amount of satisfaction that Learie used to relate the story of the meeting between an African Chief and a certain Colonial Bishop.

"Sir," said the African chief, "when you Christians came here, you had the Bible and we had the land. Now we have the Bible and you have the land." It must have been difficult for the Bishop to reply. There is no record of his answer.

Learie remembered the first time he had realised that there was a difference in the colour of people's skin. And the realisation brought with it a fear of people with white skins. He was only five years old at the time.

He and his brother had been playing ball in the yard near his parents' home. His mother, who was in the house, kept glancing out at them as though something was worrying her.

Soon there came the "clop-clop" of a horse's hooves drawing near.

"Get into the house or he'll ride over you," screamed the boys' mother as she ran protectively towards them.

Learie sensed the unusual terror in his mother's voice, and was deeply affected by it. He knew his mother to be a quiet, calm and kindly soul, usually with the sound of music in her voice, and the light of laughter in her eyes.

Now, however, there was no music in her voice, no laughter in her eyes. Terror and fear, respectively, were in their place instead.

He subsequently discovered the reason for his mother's fear. A black child who had failed to get out of the way in time had almost been trampled to death by this same white rider. It was an accident, perhaps, but it had happened nonetheless. Young as he was, from that day Learie began to realise that there were disadvantages in being black.

Strange, but before this, he had never even been aware that he and many of his young friends were black, as distinct from others who were white.

He began to look at all the people around him. There was Mr Smith, who employed his father as an overseer on his cocoa estate. Mr Smith was Learie's godfather, as kind a man as anyone could want to meet. Learie had never realised that Mr Smith was different from his father. Now the difference struck him. Mr Smith was white, while his father was black.

Black, white, black, white – even when his eyes were closed, the colours kept moving round and round before him. He could not shut them out.

"Was there no place for Negroes in the white man's world?" he asked himself as he grew up.

The history of the West Indies has been, for so long, a history of the "so-called" superiority of the white man over the coloured, that the coloured man himself, in an effort to gain recognition, has built a social ladder, the rungs of which establish a clear line of demarcation between one shade of colour and another.

Some forty years ago, Gordon Bell, writing under the pen-name of George Bernard, published a little book entitled *Wayside Sketches – Pen pictures of Barbadian Life*. In this book he devotes a chapter to 'The Communities of Barbados'. Writing about the coloured communities, he states:

"It is impossible to deal with the coloured communities of our island without making reference to the race prejudice of the whites which has been instrumental in fashioning the life of the coloured people.

This race hatred, which is described by perspicacious travellers as the bitterest example of its kind to be found anywhere in the West Indies is, however, subtle rather than acute; it is like a poison-gas attack, and the victim while sensing with a physical reality the stranglehold which it has upon him, nevertheless, finds himself powerless to fight back. There are no lynchings, and scarcely any open discrimination or Jim-Crowism is practised at public houses. The foreigner (who hasn't the time nor perhaps the inclination to make his own investigations), who enquires about racial relationships will be told there is no race question in Barbados.

". . . Over the subject of colour prejudice the local tendency is to adopt the plan of the ostrich which hides its head in the sand at the approach of danger. The existence of such a sentiment is never admitted, and its discussion is tabooed by white and black alike. The foreigner will be told very impressively that there are coloured members in our Legislature, in our Civil Service, and in the ranks of the Commissioned Officers of the Barbados Volunteer Force. And of course, he will depart with the firm impression that we are a people from whose book the Americans might profitably borrow a leaf. Those, however, who remain in the colony long enough, soon begin to sense the real state of the relationship.

"This strong feeling on colour on the part of the whites has produced an effect upon the Negro which is more demoralising by far than any other economic pressure could be. It has destroyed his faith in himself, giving him a racial inferiority complex. The result is, that the successful Negro in Barbados always takes care to marry a woman of lighter complexion than himself, partly because his bitter experience has taught him to place a premium upon a fair skin, and "partly for the sake of the children". Thus it is that we find the bitterest feelings of colour prejudice existing within the ranks of the coloured people themselves. . . . The fact that not merely class, but also tint of skin, determines one's position in the coloured communities of Barbados has created such a labyrinth of distinctions that it is utterly impossible to tell where one class begins and where another ends. Nowhere are a people so divided against themselves by barriers which they must often long to smash if they only possessed the necessary moral courage. . . ."

The writer then gives an account of each of the various classes into which the inhabitants are grouped.

What 'George Bernard' has written of Barbadian society is not peculiar to Barbados. Writers from other territories have a similar tale to tell. Racialism and colour prejudice undermine the whole structure of West Indian society.

Learie Constantine's awareness of racialism and colour prejudice within society as a whole caused him many unhappy moments.

Some – even his friends – have said that he was oversensitive where colour was concerned, and queried the necessity for this sensitivity when he himself had so many genuine friends among the whites who were willing to do anything for him.

But like Paul Robeson, the famous American Negro singer, who objected to the fact that doors which were open to him were shut in the faces of other members of his race, Learie felt that to close his eyes to the injustices meted out to other coloured folk would be a betrayal of his people.

He welcomed the hand of friendship extended to

him, but always, lurking in the depths of his mind, was the New Testament thought, "Inasmuch as ye did it not to one of the least of my brethren, ye did it not to me."

Throughout his life, his faith in the coloured man never wavered, and in *Colour Bar*, he set out to give the Negro's view of the black and white problem.

"While I was writing this book," he penned, "a white man and a coloured man together climbed the highest peak in the world. There are no heights to which we cannot rise . . . together."

His suggested solution to the colour bar problem was – LOVE!

10 West Indian captaincy

The old order changeth, yielding place to new.

Morte D'Arthur Tennyson

For many long years, the question of West Indian captaincy was a sore point with coloured West Indian cricketers. That Learie felt strongly in the matter is evidenced by his writing in *Cricket in the Sun.*

"I think the time has come," he wrote, "to speak out plainly what I mean in this matter of West Indian captaincy. It is not only what I mean – every coloured player who has ever turned out in an intercolonial side has been conscious of it, and it rots the heart out of cricket, and always will until it is changed."

Learie was never, during his entire cricketing career which spanned almost two decades, to captain a West Indian Test side at Lord's, Sydney, Bourda, or the Queen's Park Oval in his native Trinidad. The distinction of leading a West Indies team on tour was to be accorded another gifted West Indian player – the Barbadian Sir Frank Worrell – and this was to be achieved only after a fiery and vigorous Press campaign in which that doughty fighter and notable authority on cricket in all its aspects, C. L. R. James, played a prominent part. James was at the time editor of the weekly newspaper, *The Nation*, organ of the ruling People's National Movement of Trinidad and Tobago, and he wielded, therefore, tremendous influence. It was surely ironic that as far back as 1945 – fifteen years before Worrell took over the West Indian captaincy – Learie had been considered worthy of assuming the leadership of a Dominions' Eleven at Lord's. Truly, this prophet was to gain little honour among his own countrymen! So far at least as the cricket captaincy was concerned!

The very first visit of a West Indian Cricket team to England took place in 1900. The team was captained by Aucher Warner, a brother of the more famous Sir Pelham ('Plum') Warner, one of the greatest names in the history of the game. Aucher Warner, a Trinidadian by birth and, like his brother, a first-rate player, was an obvious choice for the captaincy, in the absence of H. B. G. Austin. There could have been absolutely no question as to his capabilities for the task.

The same applied to the captaincy of the 1906 and 1923 West Indian touring sides which were led by the late H. B. G. Austin. Austin, who was also a Major in the British Army, was a member of a distinguished white Barbadian family, and is generally acknowledged to be one of the founding fathers of West Indian cricket. He saw active service in South Africa, which caused him to miss the 1900 English tour. Austin was an accomplished player, who merited by right his place on the team. He was a highly efficient administrator, and his knowledge of the game was immense. Constantine has confessed publicly on more than one occasion his very considerable debt to Major Austin, and James in his *Beyond A Boundary* has stated in unequivocal terms that "H. B. G. Austin was the natural captain of the West Indies as long as he chose to play."

By 1928, however, Austin was off the scene and, meanwhile, many extremely talented coloured players, apart from Constantine, had arisen. Out of these a captain could surely have been found who would have been quite capable of leading a touring side, in any quarter of the globe, with ability and the necessary dignity. The controversy over the West Indian captaincy dates really from this period. It became a burning question and remained a sore point for upwards of thirty years. It had an unhealthy effect, too, upon the game and resulted in a souring of relationships on various occasions. As was perhaps inevitable, West Indian cricket had entered the region of politics, assuming sometimes many of the uglier aspects that such a development invariably signifies.

What was Learie's attitude towards this vital and, often, agitating question?

In some respects his attitude differed from the view as expressed by his friend and colleague C. L. R. James. Learie felt, and he repeated it forcefully in and out of season, that in a predominantly coloured community and with representative cricket teams composed for the most part of coloured players, the captain should by right be a man of colour. He never wavered from that standpoint. James, on the other hand, while by no means blind to that aspect of the matter, was firmly of the opinion that a West Indian captain should not necessarily be a black man, or a coloured man, but the best possible man for the job. If the best available person happened to be a black man, as was undoubtedly the case when the issue facing the selectors was a choice between Frank Worrell and Gerry Alexander, all the better. As indicated earlier, James waged a relentless battle on behalf of Worrell for the captaincy of the 1960–61 West Indian touring team to Australia. As he wrote subsequently, "My argument was simply this; there was not the slightest shadow of justification for Alexander to be captain of a side in which Frank Worrell was playing." It might be well to add in this place that Worrell was fully to justify the confidence placed in him, and to establish himself securely as one of the greatest of Test captains anywhere.

Sir Learie Constantine with West Indies Test captain Frank Worrell, at a lunch given in 1963 by British Prime Minister Harold Macmillan in honour of the West Indies and English Test captains

There were powerful arguments on both sides, and Constantine's outlook was understandable, especially in a period when colonialism was still dominant throughout the West Indian islands. It was increasingly being felt by many zealous supporters of the game, who would never have questioned the capacity of such men as Warner and Austin, that under existing circumstances it was evident that the white (or lighter-skinned) communities in whom economic power reposed, were really holding on to the tradition of *white* captaincy with the primary aim of using it as a political weapon against the progressive forces that were emerging in West Indian society. A West Indian Test side, that in the eyes of the world could only be captained capably by a white man – and the whites were the minority group – offered convincing evidence of the black man's unfitness to govern himself. Prejudice can always find apparently valid reasons for preserving the *status quo*.

It was equally clear that for as long as it was practicable, the more reactionary among the ruling classes would see to it that the old policy was maintained. Therefore, R. K. Nunes, a white Jamaican and former Dulwich schoolboy, was appointed to skipper the 1928 team to tour England, despite protests. His selection, Learie argued, was a debatable one and did not produce good results. Similarly, when in 1930 the West Indies team was due to sail for Australia, the youthful G. C. Grant, fresh from his studies at Cambridge, "met the side in the West Indies to take it across the Pacific." As Learie commented, rather bitterly, in *Cricket in the Sun*, "It is no disparagement of him to say that whatever they taught him at Cambridge it could not have been our respective merits as part of a team, because the same might have been said of anyone else who was as new to us as he was."

It was G. C. ('Jackie') Grant who also led the 1933 West Indian side to England, a disappointing tour in many respects. "We were more like a mob," wrote Learie, adding, "Grant did his best, but he did not know us well enough. He might not even have known the game well enough; but that is a personal opinion."

Despite these setbacks which served to show up the situation in all its ghastliness, the captaincy of the 1939 team to England was given to Grant's younger brother, Rolph Grant, who was at the time more renowned as an amateur goalkeeper for the English Corinthians Club. Rolph Grant was, it is needless to add, even less experienced for the task than his brother, but he proved himself undeniably to be a very brilliant fieldsman, and some of his performances are still remembered. This 1939 tour was brought to a premature end by the War. As a matter of interest, it might be pointed out that, between these years 1928 to 1939, the various West Indian touring sides could boast of the presence of such brilliant non-white players as C. A. Roach, H. C. Griffith, Errol Hunte, Derek Sealy, Ellis Achong, Ben Sealey, Learie Constantine, George Headley, the brothers W. and E. St Hill, Joe Small, F. R. Martin, and V. A. Valentine, to mention only a few. Many of these men, as was well known, were of sound education and had excellent social backgrounds. In addition, there were many coloured men who had captained intercolonial cricket teams with distinction and complete competence. Names like the late André Cipriani (Trinidad) and C. R. Browne (British Guiana), both of them barristers as well as outstanding cricketers, immediately spring to mind.

With these obvious examples in mind, it was not surprising that Learie always held the firm conviction that a black, or coloured, man would eventually take over the more responsible post of West Indian cricket captain and, not only that, would lend grace and lustre to it. He made the further prediction – his fingers were always on the pulse of the times – that this event would take place during his lifetime. It was, therefore, extremely gratifying, especially to those who had always shared his views, that he did live to see his prophecy fulfilled when, in 1960, the mantle fell upon the shoulders of the suave and polished Frank Worrell. He had always known that the hour would come!

Learie was never narrow in his views on race. He could, for example, confess at a political meeting to a profound admiration for the works of Rudyard Kipling, even though he disliked what Kipling stood for – the "white man's burden" and the "lesser breeds without the law" and all the rest of the Empire-building stuff. He was, and remained throughout his life, strongly critical of all forms of racial discrimination. Unlike some later nationalists, however, he was not ungrateful for the manner in which he had been received and treated by the public of Britain and the Commonwealth at large. He wanted to see more and more doors opened to the other members of his race. Hence his apparent bitterness at times, which puzzled some people.

Ultimately, once the right of all men to equal treatment and equal opportunities in all spheres of activity had been accorded, irrespective of race, it is not improbable that Learie would have come round to his friend C. L. R. James's view of the matter. The right man for the post, any post, should always be the best and most qualified man, the particular shade of complexion being of no importance.

For, is it not a characteristic feature of the various Caribbean islands that they are made up essentially of mixed communities, where people of all races are privileged to meet and mingle? It is, perhaps, in communities such as these that the very determination of mankind's future will eventually lie – communities in which the Warners and Austins, the Constantines and

Challenors, the Grants and Worrells, the Stollmeyers and Sobers' and Atkinsons shall, it is confidently hoped, all find an equal place.

11 Do so ain't like so

Oh wad some Pow'r the giftie gi'e us
To see oursels as ithers see us.

To a Mouse Robert Burns

In the West Indies there is a common expression, "Do so ain't like so", which simply refers to the fact that there are those who consider it quite in order to do to others what they object to having others do to them.

Learie was amazed to find that even in the world of cricket the "do-so-ain't-like-so" policy often obtained. Much has been written about bodyline bowling. Bitter has been the reaction to it at times – more bitter at some times than at others. Learie admitted to having himself shortened the ball now and then, on the advice of his captain, from as far back as 1924. The object was to get out a few good batsmen who were giving trouble. There was no harm meant, and when the batsmen refused to be intimidated, but played the ball however Learie bowled it, there was no harm done.

Hewetson, the Warwickshire fast bowler, in the 1923 England v West Indies game, had shortened the ball on the leg side when trying to get Tarilton of Barbados out. He had succeeded. Learie had taken note. George John used the same tactics from time to time. Learie considered the use of the short ball as a legitimate weapon in the bowler's attack on "the enemy". Deliberately bowling to hurt a batsman, however, was an abuse of the weapon, and this Learie did not condone.

In 1928, when Learie toured England with West

Indies for the second time, Larwood deliberately bumped the balls down. The West Indies' batsmen dealt with such bowling to the best of their ability, *but no one complained.*

When, during the same tour, Learie occasionally bowled a bumper, Hobbs and Jardine had much to say against his method. Strangely enough, however, when Larwood, bowling against West Indies at Lord's later, almost knocked one or two of the men out, Jardine saw nothing wrong. And it was the same Jardine who, in 1932–33, caused all the bodyline hullabaloo in Australia when, as captain, he instructed Larwood to knock the Australians about. Protest from the other side had little influence over him. Two hundred policemen, all armed, had to keep order during one of the Tests.

In 1930, Bill Voce was a member of the M.C.C. team which visited the West Indies. *He* bowled bodyline at times, even knocking Inniss out cold, but no one in the West Indies team complained. Roach and Learie were among those who did the best they could to play whatever balls Voce sent down. As far as they were concerned, and as far, apparently, as the England side were concerned, that was a part of playing cricket.

When the situation was reversed in a later game in the same Test, and Learie, in an effort to draw the game, bowled right outside the leg stump, Calthorpe of the England team publicly accused Learie of bowling that was "not cricket".

The matter did not end there. Prior to the next Test, the team manager of the English side approached Learie with the request that he bowl fewer leg-side bumpers, since the English batsmen felt that he was trying to injure them. Nothing was further from Learie's mind than injuring anyone. Nevertheless, in good spirit, he agreed. Imagine his surprise, and the surprise of others of the West Indies team, who batted first, when Voce sent balls whizzing wildly round their heads.

"What is sauce for the goose is sauce for the gander" was apparently not applicable in the minds of the M.C.C. team.

If the eyes of Australia and the world were centred on England and Jardine and Larwood during the much talked about Australian tour, the M.C.C. and the rest of England centred *their* eyes on Constantine during the 1933 West Indies tour of England. At Lord's in May, Patsy Hendren created a sensation by turning out on the field in a crash helmet! When Learie was bowling, Patsy wore a thickly padded cricket cap, his temples and ears being well covered with the peaks of two other caps. The insinuation was evident, but hardly to be expected from a team that knew how it felt to be accused of deliberately hurting others.

When West Indies batted, and George Headley was knocked out for more than five minutes (not, mark you, by one of his own team!) Learie and the others thought it might not be a bad idea to borrow Patsy's helmet. They refrained from doing so, however, fearing the possible failure of the English to take such an action in the same spirit in which West Indies had taken Hendren's appearance.

It was far too obvious that England was one-sided on the question of what is good enough in cricket. For them, everything seemed to depend on who was affected at the time. Surely, "not cricket", this!

Neville Cardus, in an essay on Harold Larwood, published in *The Playfair Cardus* (1963), makes reference to the Australian summer of 1932–33 when

"Larwood, acting under the unflinching generalship of Douglas Jardine, threatened to split in twain the Commonwealth of cricket. To reduce the runs and moral ascendancy of Bradman the attack called 'body-line' was invented, and put into brilliant and devastating execution, mainly by Larwood. But back in England Larwood was frowned on whenever he gave our own batsmen a taste of Jardine's medicine. Certain county clubs broke off relations with Nottinghamshire. Photos were taken and exhibited of the bruised empurpled anatomies of English batsmen, lately colleagues of Larwood in the land of the barbarians – meaning Australia – photos of English ribs tickled by Larwood, who could not make the proper British compromise and realise that what was good and fair for Bradman could not possibly be served up to our own thoroughbred gentlemen."

West Indian temperament also has often come under fire from the Englishman. The West Indian is accused of having his feelings lie too near the surface. He laughs heartily when there is something to laugh about, it is true. He is sad when things are not as they should be. Is he unique in such manifestations of feeling? Have not English players been known to show their feelings too, regardless of their reputation for imperturbability? Learie in his time saw famous white players in tears, and thought no less of them because of that. Certainly in football, another popular English sport, the players show no restraint. They hug each other joyfully when their side scores a goal. They are more West Indian then than the West Indian himself. *He that is without sin, let him first cast a stone.*

In 1960 an exasperated West Indian crowd threw bottles on the cricket field at Queen's Park Oval, Trinidad. The umpire (a West Indian one!) had given a questionable decision in favour of the M.C.C. The violence of the crowd was noised abroad. No right-thinking person, be he English or West Indian, condoned such violence. But did this violence in any way exceed – or even equate with – the violence that follows an English football match ? It is so easy to see the mote in another's eye while we overlook the beam in our own.

In one respect at least, England has not changed much since Learie's earlier cricketing days. West Indies' 1973 summer tour of England has undoubtedly proved that. How Learie would have shaken his head had he been sitting in the pavilion at Edgbaston or the Long Room at Lord's! He would surely have been tempted to talk out concerning the situation then. And he would just as surely have succumbed to the temptation.

Others, normally less vocal than he where injustice is concerned, have not been able to hold their peace. The one-sidedness of the English sportswriters and commentators was far too blatant on this occasion to escape notice and comment.

To have ignored the outpourings of E. M. Wellings of the *Evening News* might have been the best course for the average West Indian reader to pursue. Such bias is typical of E. M. Wellings! But when similar biased reporting of matches came from quarters from which one least expected it, that was too much to swallow.

England's image in the sporting world has suffered in the eyes of West Indies if not in her own. Evidently, as far as England was concerned, it was unsportsmanlike of the West Indies to insist on winning the series, and winning it in the same manner as England, placed in similar circumstances, would have won.

"England expects every man to do his duty", and it

is the duty (and the prerogative too, it seems) of the English cricketer either to *win* matches or to *save* them, no matter how bored the spectators might be by the tactics which they use. On the other hand, it is the duty of the West Indian cricketer to play bright cricket, to keep the paying crowds coming, no matter the outcome of the game. Or so, at least, England seems to think!

At Edgbaston that summer West Indies played cricket as the English play it. 3 wickets for 39, 5 wickets for 128; no chances taken, no chances given! 190 runs scored by the end of the first day's play. How the English press lambasted them for slow scoring – the *same* press that saw England score 169 on the third day, and said not a word about it! What must "the lesser breeds without the law" think? One rule for England, another for West Indies, all in the same game!

West Indies' captain Kanhai was the object of severe criticism because of "ungentlemanly behaviour" when Boycott was appealed against unsuccessfully. Did the same critics remember their own Illingworth's behaviour in Australia during the M.C.C. tour there not so long before? What was his reaction to the decisions of umpire Rowan?

The final straw to break the camel's back is taken from *The Daily Telegraph's* editorial of August 28 when the series was over. "The West Indians must pause to consider the example they are setting." Should this not have read: "The West Indians must pause to consider whether the English example which they are *following* is a good one."

Constantine, in the concluding chapter of *Cricket in the Sun* wrote, "At last I have said those things openly which have (been) muttered and echoed round the dressing-rooms for years, and which I have heard so often accompanied by the remark, 'If only somebody would say that we think straight out, I wonder if it would better things?' and snuffed by the reply, 'And what would the M.C.C. say to that?'"

"I hope the M.C.C. will say something to it now that they have the chance. For I, like the M.C.C., have the future of the game deeply at heart; I, like them, want to weed out whatever spoils cricket and makes it unfair or dull."

Double standards undoubtedly spoil cricket.

Whither, therefore, England and cricket, unless they change their "do-so-ain't-like-so" policy? West Indies will not remain silent for ever. That is clear. Another Constantine, and another, will arise!

12 The war years

On the idle hill of summer,
Sleepy with the flow of streams,
Far I hear the steady drummer
Drumming like a noise in dreams.

Far and near and low and louder
On the roads of earth go by,
Dear to friends and food for powder,
Soldiers marching, all to die.

A Shropshire Lad A. E. Housman

It was a British novelist, the late W. B. Maxwell, a favourite with readers of a past generation, who described the War of 1914–18 as "The Great Interruption". The phrase was an appropriate one and provides us also with a very apt description of the Second World War (1939–45) which interrupted numerous things and proved almost a death-blow to the game of cricket. The war years had their effect on Learie's life and brought to a premature end his career as a Test player. There was unfortunately to be no crowning glory at the close. As Learie has pointed out somewhere, a cricketer who has passed the *ripe* age of thirty-five soon learns that there is a lessening demand for his services. In 1939, Learie was already in his thirty-eighth year, but he had earned a place, nevertheless, on the West Indian side that was touring England that summer. It was to be his last appearance for the West Indies. The imminent outbreak of hostilities brought the tour to an abrupt end. The rest of the team returned home hurriedly, but Learie remained in England, where he and his family spent the entire war period. By the time peace came in 1945, his career in international cricket was over. During those fateful years when a world tragedy was being enacted, Learie engaged in League cricket for a time, and even on one memorable occasion captained a Dominions side in a charity match at Lord's, but his Test days were now definitely behind him. The situation produced by the war had an adverse effect also on the Test careers of such fellow West Indians as Ellis Achong and 'Manny' Martindale. Truly, a great interruption indeed!

Learie had been particularly keen to be a member of this 1939 visiting West Indian team. Although, so far as he was concerned, it would probably mean for him some financial loss (he was at the time earning £800 for a twenty-week spell with Rochdale) Learie confessed that his secret ambition was to play a part in contributing towards a West Indian victory in a Test series against England, a victory that he hoped would be accomplished at last by his countrymen away from their homeland. Because of this, he wanted the best possible side to be selected, and one that would be strongly supported by the cream of those West Indian professional players who were at the time resident in England. It was through an intermediary – Mr R. H. Mallett, an Englishman – that Learie commenced negotiations on this and other matters with the West Indies Cricket Board. Mr Mallett was a member of the M.C.C. The negotiations were prolonged and were only partially successful. Learie was finally told that, as regards the important question of the fees he was requesting for his professional services, everything would depend upon the financial results of the tour. The tour's sudden termination naturally put an end to all his hopes and expectations, but he thoroughly enjoyed the cricket while it lasted, despite the atrocious English weather which made it difficult for the newcomers especially to acclimatise themselves to the prevailing conditions. "It was a blue-faced and shivering mob," Learie has written, "which stepped thankfully off the boat in 1939, and once they were here the weather moved steadily back towards mid-winter."

There were other respects, however, in which 1939, despite its grimness and ultimate tragedy, proved to be a memorable year for Learie. It was in this year that he had his first experience of playing for Windhill in the Bradford League of Yorkshire. He found the organisation of this League to be superb. Also, unlike the case with the various other Leagues, each club was entitled under its constitution to employ as many as four professionals. Elsewhere, only one professional player per club was usually engaged. In Learie's opinion, the practices obtainable in this Bradford League were accountable in large measure for the strength and vitality of Yorkshire cricket, and provided an explanation as to why that County so often emerged as the County Cricket champions. The League was at all times on the look-out for players of promise and rendered them, when discovered, every assistance and encouragement. That was why, according to Learie, the war made no difference whatsoever to the 'spirit' of Yorkshire cricket. "In the Bradford League," Learie has stated in *Cricket in the Sun*, "one club after another signed some of the greatest players in the country." Among these were such names as Hobbs, Woolley, and Sydney Barnes; Voce, Gunn, and Leyland, as well as the West Indians Martindale and Achong.

"These are players," Learie again wrote, "who have appeared regularly before Yorkshire crowds, and whose style has been sedulously learned and copied by Yorkshiremen and boys who will, in the future, emulate them to the discomfort of cricket counties farther south."

Learie's days as a serious and dedicated professional cricketer were fast approaching their end, however.

War-time cricket.

England was at war, and never for one moment wavering in his resolve, he felt that he must sink or swim with her. He had no intention of deserting, in her hour of peril and greatest need, the country which had been extremely generous to him in many respects. Already, Nelson – with which his name will always be associated – had become his permanent place of residence. Having arrived eventually at the decision to retire from professional cricket, the law still remaining his ultimate goal, he obtained employment as an equipment clerk in the Air Raid Precautions Department of the Nelson Borough Council. He was also appointed a Billeting Officer, his duties being to find accommodation for servicemen who were stationed in the Nelson area.

Learie performed both of these jobs satisfactorily, and it was not long before the value of the work he had done was recognised by the British Government. He received the appointment of Welfare Officer for the Ministry of Labour and National Service in the North West Region of England. His activities now were for the most part centred in Liverpool. The job proved to be a very challenging one and offered the fullest scope for his particular talents. It was a source of considerable satisfaction to him that the post he occupied enabled him to be of service to his own countrymen.

A fairly large number of coloured West Indians had come to Britain in response to a call to replace British workers in industry who were being called up. Learie soon discovered that recruitment of this labour force had not been very well planned. Many of the men were in fact unskilled and quite unused to conditions in such a highly industrialised area as the North of England. To add to the difficulties of the situation, there was the thorny and delicate problem of race and colour. It was very fortunate for these men that their Welfare Officer should be such a man as Learie, fortified as he was by his years of experience of life in England. His name and prestige were also of considerable value. Learie faced up to the situation manfully. He was able to offer sound advice to the men and to assist them also in finding suitable lodgings. One of the men's chief complaints was that they were expected to accept wages which were lower than the wages they had been promised. As a means of correcting this, Learie found an answer by initiating training schemes which would enable them to acquire as soon as possible the necessary skills. He did his best at the same time to allay the suspicions of employers, on the one hand, and to curb the resentment of some of the white employees, on the other. He needed all the tact at his command to accomplish these aims. There were, for example, certain firms that had refused to employ coloured workers. Learie's solution to this ticklish question was to induce his Ministry to press for the urgent delivery of orders. In the face of such pressure, especially in wartime, it was not long before the unofficial ban against coloured workers was lifted. His untiring efforts did not go unrewarded. The gratitude of the men for all that he had done for them was to be manifested at a later period, and in calmer times.

During the course of his duties with the Ministry in Liverpool, Learie also learned that race prejudice existed in quarters where it was least to be expected. He had close relations over a fairly long period with the then Anglican Bishop of Liverpool, the late Dr David. Learie had admitted that in all matters pertaining to business, he was treated with the utmost courtesy and consideration by the Bishop. On the question of colour segregation, however, Dr David, in other respects a "tolerant and kindly man" remained "inflexible". Learie commented with some bitterness, "Like so many men who gain a reputation for usefulness in the colour problem, all he appeared to want from it was the ability to segregate white and coloured, and to keep the coloured people sufficiently fed and clothed and housed perhaps, but definitely 'in their place'."

During these years he was privileged to make several broadcasts, and he appeared on the BBC 'Brains Trust' programme in company with several distinguished British intellectuals like Dr Julian Huxley and others.

He did a good deal of lecturing to Army, Navy, and R.A.F. personnel who were stationed in North West England. His zeal and enthusiasm for the task in hand never faltered. To his numerous admirers, therefore, it came as no surprise when, in recognition of his services, he received, in 1946, the award of M.B.E. from His Majesty King George VI. Much as he appreciated this honour conferred upon him, Learie took even greater pride in the illuminated scroll he had received from the men with whom he had worked, and whose cause he had championed, during those strenuous and at times heart-breaking years.

13 Family life

And they twain shall be one flesh: so then they are no more twain, but one flesh: St Mark 10:8

The dedication in Learie's book *Cricket in the Sun* reads thus:

To
MY WIFE
Who has a husband in winter
But who has been comrade, adviser, and inspiration
summer and winter alike

This sums up briefly the pattern of Learie Constantine's family life over a number of years. Norma, his wife, and Gloria, his daughter, had learned to live without his physical presence for the greater part of each year.

Prior to her marriage to Learie, Norma Cox, as she was then, had found it difficult to "play second fiddle" to cricket. She lived in the city. Learie lived in the country, and worked in Port of Spain. He travelled to and from work by train, and the last train left the city at 7 p.m. On evenings after work, Learie would hurry to the nets to practise for as long as possible. The longer he practised, the less time it left for him to spend with Norma before he had to hurry off to catch the train home.

Things went on like this for a time, until Norma felt that she could tolerate the situation no longer. She issued an ultimatum to Learie.

"Make your choice! It's either cricket or me!"

He pleaded earnestly with her.

"Don't make it difficult for me," he begged. "Please let it be cricket *and* you. I don't want to give up either."

Looking back on those days, Norma often smiled at the memory of how completely bowled over she had been by his request. She had acquiesced. Instead of allowing herself to feel jealous, she began to take a keener interest in his cricket. She and Learie were eventually married on the 25th of July, 1927.

"You'll never regret this," he promised. She never did.

When Learie went to Lancashire in 1929 to take up his first appointment as professional with the Nelson Cricket Club, Norma accompanied him, but their infant daughter was left behind in Trinidad with her grandparents.

The difficulties of those early months, when as strangers in Nelson they had no one else but each other to turn to for company or comfort, served more than anything else to draw them closer together in a bond which was never afterwards broken. It was a long time before any neighbour even looked through a window to exchange "Good-morning" with them. When he left the cricket field, Norma was all that Learie had.

With her he shared the funny side of life. In the early days she had been amused by his seemingly serious assertion that on many an occasion he had bowled an English cricketer out, and the latter had walked to the pavilion and turned and walked straight back out to the wicket again. Englishmen had seemed all alike to him!

It was to Norma, too, that he poured out his doubts and fears, his joys and sorrows. She became his source of strength. When he was despondent, it was she who cheered him up. He always attributed to her the fact that he stayed on in Nelson after their first two years there.

Often he received abusive letters, asking him why he did not go back to his own country; and these letters made him sad. In this unhappy situation, Norma had enjoined, "Let us turn and fight it. In the end they will realise that basically we are just like them, and they will accept us in spite of our colour." Her words proved true.

C. L. R. James, in his book *Beyond a Boundary* was able to relate an incident which bore testimony to the fact that by 1932 the Constantine family had been recognised as citizens of Nelson.

During the time that James stayed at the home of Learie and Norma, a friend turned up one morning for a chat and a cup of tea. As she was leaving, she turned to Norma and said that she was just going to do her own shopping, and that she would be willing to do Norma's too, if the latter had not yet done it.

Some time after the friend had left, Learie pointed out to James what a nasty day it was outside. "Her offer to do Norma's shopping," he explained, "was just to save Norma from going out on a day like this. That is really why she came."

The Constantines had at last been drawn into the circle.

Learie's return to the West Indies after his first stint as professional at Nelson was followed by an invitation to play cricket in New York. This tour was organised by a group of West Indians living in New York. Norma was invited to accompany him. At the end of the engagement, Learie received an honorarium, but he took back with him also the memory of a wonderful catch which he had made in one match, and the resulting swarming of the pitch by spectators who rained coins and notes upon him. Norma was silent when she saw in his eyes the look that indicated that he was trying to shut out the memory of something less spectacular, but could she blame him? After having been advertised as "the fastest bowler in the world, and a harder hitter than Gilbert Jessop", it must have been a blow to his pride to have scored 1 in his first innings and 4 in his second. But such are the ups and downs of cricket!

When Learie went back to Nelson for his second season, little Gloria accompanied her parents. The family was now complete. Years before, Learie had visualised himself coaching a son of his at cricket, just as his father had coached him, but this was never to be. Gloria remained their only child. If Learie did not have the privilege of seeing a son of his play cricket, at least his daughter, as she grew up, had the pleasure of watching him, and feeling proud of his achievements, for Norma always took Gloria along to see all the big matches in which her father played.

Although in the beginning she was too young to appreciate what was going on, nevertheless Gloria still knew how to enjoy herself. Some of the friends of the family recall the little girl tirelessly jumping up and down the steps of the pavilion while many a match was in progress.

When she was five years old, Gloria was sent to the Nelson Preparatory School, of which Miss Washington was the Headmistress. She was the only coloured child there. At that age, however, this caused no particular problems. She was happy there. The problems developed as she grew older.

The only unpleasant incident which stands out in her memory of Miss Washington's school had nothing to do with colour, and it did not at the time seem to end too unpleasantly, in Gloria's opinion.

One day another little child slapped her. As a result, she went home in floods of tears. When her mother found out the cause of the tears, she advised Gloria against being a cry-baby.

"You must learn to fight back," she said.

This was the same advice she had often given to her husband when he had had problems, and it had worked. Little Gloria, confident that she had her mother's backing, returned to school, sought out the offender, and promptly walloped her. Mrs Constantine had not intended that her advice should have been taken so literally, but it served its purpose. No other child ever slapped Gloria again.

Her next school was the Convent of Our Lady of Lourdes in the neighbouring town, Colne. She spent the years 1935 to 1939 at the Convent, and it was during this period that Gloria began to realise that she was 'different'. All the other girls wore their hair cut short, with a bang, as the fashion was then. Her mother insisted on combing hers in four plaits. Gloria hated this. What made matters worse was when an enterprising geography teacher, trying to make vivid her illustration of the Nile delta, called Gloria up before the class and pointed to her head, and the partings between her plaits.

On being told of the incident, Mrs Constantine for once lost her usual equanimity. She failed to see the aptness of the illustration, the ingenuity of the teacher's spontaneous action, or the justification for the embarrassment which she felt it must have caused her daughter. She went to the school, and protested vigorously to the nun in charge, who promptly apologised and gave her the assurance that no harm was meant.

The incident did not in any way help to improve Gloria's attitude to the hated plaits. Years later, when asked why, if she so hated the way her mother combed her hair, she had not learnt to comb it herself, she replied, "It is easier to practise on someone else's head. Where would I have found another child with hair like mine?"

As she grew older, Gloria had to deal with her share of the colour problem. Once a white boy spat in her face. The unexpectedness of his action left her momentarily stunned. By the time she had recovered her faculties, he was no longer anywhere in sight. Gloria made up her mind how she would deal with him if ever she should see him again. Fortunately, for his sake, she never did. He was not one of her school-mates.

At that time, the Constantine family was living in Meredith Street, in the Borough of Nelson. When the war clouds broke in 1939, bringing to a premature end the West Indies tour of England, Learie, who had been a member of the West Indies team, returned to Nelson to be with his family and to offer his services to the country in which he had resided for the past ten years. Mrs Constantine and Gloria had been holidaying in Europe that summer, and had taken the last boat out of Ostend before war was actually declared.

When Learie was appointed Welfare Officer in Liverpool, he lived in a hostel just outside the town during the week, but he returned home for weekends – every weekend in the beginning, and later, not quite so frequently. He owned a car which he used for his work in Liverpool, but petrol rationing forced him to travel to Nelson by train.

As her contribution to the war effort, Mrs Constantine became a member of the St John's Ambulance Brigade. Grim as the war years were, they still held moments of pleasure which the Constantine family shared together. Sunday matches for the benefit of the Red Cross and other charitable institutions were played regularly during those years, and very often, Learie took his wife and daughter along to watch while he played in the one-day games. They enjoyed these outings immensely, and for a while almost succeeded in forgetting that there was such a thing as a war.

Throughout all his years as a cricketer, previous to the war, Learie firmly believed in the value of proper training. He used to run two to three miles a day, he jogged, pulled strands, and watched his diet. He never ate lunch during matches. He took only something to drink, and had his main meal after a match. He did not smoke, nor did he drink alcohol.

During the war years, however, he was persuaded to drink sherry. "You may not live until tomorrow," his friends pointed out. Laughingly, Learie quaffed his sherry. Cricket and wine lightened the horrors of Hitler's mad attacks on a world which had hitherto been striving to retain its sanity.

The war held no special terrors for the teenager Gloria. The noise of bombs seemed far away from Nelson. Although there were air raid shelters near their home, the Constantine family never made use of them.

"If we must die," said Learie, "let us die above the ground. Eventually, it will be for a long, long time that we shall be below."

From the Convent of Our Lady of Lourdes, Gloria had gone next to the Nelson Grammar School. She spent the war years there. Nelson Grammar School was a co-educational school, and here again she was the only coloured student. Soon she was being called by the nickname 'Blackout'. Gloria ignored it, and after a while all name-calling ceased. Before she left

Family group

the grammar school she had become so popular with her teachers and classmates that she was elected to be a prefect and a house captain. The senior mistress chose the prefects, while the pupils themselves elected their house captains.

On her own merit, Gloria had earned her place in the community, just as her parents before her had done. What she does not particularly like to be reminded of nowadays (and close friends of the family who themselves lived in Nelson during her girlhood like to talk about it still) is the fact that, listening to a group of students coming noisily down the streets, they could never distinguish which voice was Gloria's. She had as pure a Lancashire accent as any of the other children. She was truly one of them!

After the war was over in 1945, two-thirds of all University places were reserved for the men and women who had served Britain, the remaining one third of places going to students fresh from school. To merit one of these places was therefore no mean achievement. Learie and Norma had every reason to be proud of their daughter when, on graduating from grammar school in 1946, she was accepted at St Andrew's University in Scotland.

In 1949 the Constantine family moved to London. After a lapse of almost twenty years, Learie had started to study again – this time for the Bar exams, and he wanted to be near the Inns of Court. When in the 1930s he had tried to resume his studies to be a solicitor, C. L. R. James, who was then his house guest, had been helping him to prepare for an examination. After a while, however, Learie had had to give up the idea. He found that professional cricket and studying were like water and oil. They did not mix. His cricket suffered. Time after time he failed to score. At first he had tried to shrug the situation off, but then it became all too evident that it was getting him down. He was pensive and glum. He was forced to admit defeat and give up studying. Gradually he regained his cricket form and could smile again.

Now that his cricketing days were over, he should more easily be able to concentrate on studying. He still continued to give lectures and B.B.C. broadcasts. Although he had had no extensive formal education, Learie was well-read, and spoke fluently on a variety of subjects. This fact surprised quite a number of persons who tended to think of him as a cricketer only. On hearing that he was to give a talk on Shakespeare, someone was heard to remark, "What does *he* know about Shakespeare?" How little did that person know about Learie!

With all the good intentions that Learie had, it did not take Norma long to realise that there was still a major obstacle to be overcome if her husband was to study undisturbed. The constant stream of visitors to see him must be stopped. Some were friends whom Learie always welcomed heartily in spite of the inroads their visits made on his study time. Others were merely sycophants. The friends, Norma felt, would understand, and the sycophants did not matter. For years the latter had tried to use Learie for their own benefit, and Norma had quickly learnt to recognise them. She was never anything but polite to them, but the blank expression on her face, and the particular look which appeared in her eyes revealed that she saw through them all. With Learie it was more difficult to tell that he knew their genuine friends from the others. He was hearty and jovial with one and all.

Apart from the adverse effect that entertaining had on Learie's studies, there was also the question of the amount of dishwashing in which Norma and Gloria became involved after the departure of the guests, since they had no domestic help.

At one stage, the mother and daughter decided to make a count of the endless stream of persons who had to be entertained. When at the end of a three-week spell, the count had reached one hundred, they decided to call it off. If things were going to continue in that way, they might as well conserve their energy and get on with the washing-up.

Norma decided that something definitely had to be done. There was to be no more entertaining. Learie must study. She took positive action in the matter. She promptly locked him in his bedroom for seven hours every day, and no visitors were allowed.

When asked whether Learie did not object to such imprisonment, Norma simply laughed.

"He has had a good innings," she said.

And she recalled the numerous times when Learie had unexpectedly brought guests home to lunch or dinner, and she had had to rise to the occasion. Fortunately, she was a good cook and her ingenuity at making appetising dishes out of next to nothing had stood her in good stead.

"Did it never occur to you that you should have put *him* in the kitchen when he brought home guests in that way?" someone asked. "That would surely have taught him a lesson!"

Norma shook her head. "I don't think it would really have mattered, because he was a good cook himself. I get one day a year off from my culinary duties. That is Boxing Day when Learie himself takes over the kitchen."

"And what a meal he can produce!" she added.

Norma's scheme worked. When in 1954 Learie

qualified as a barrister-at-law, and thereby achieved a long-standing ambition of his, again it was to Norma that he attributed much of his success. Her quiet faith in him, and her determination to see him through, had helped immeasurably. He returned to Trinidad and took up a position as Assistant Legal Adviser to Trinidad Leaseholds, the same company with which he had worked many years before.

1954 was the same year, too, in which Gloria was married to André Valere, a Trinidadian whom she had met in London some years before. The wedding took place in Trinidad in December. Mrs Constantine had travelled down from London in September to assist with preparations for the occasion, but Learie did not arrive until just shortly before the big day. For a time Gloria had had fears that she would have to walk up the aisle on the arm of someone other than her father. She was relieved when he did arrive.

"What were you worried about?" Learie asked calmly. "Have I ever let down my little girl?"

Some years later, a son was born to André and Gloria. They named him Maurice André Constantine. Norma had the pleasure of seeing him before Learie. At the time they were residing in London again, but Norma had gone across to Trinidad to be with Gloria for the event. What proud grandparents they were! When eventually Learie first saw Maurice, the latter was an eighteen-month old toddler. As Learie held the little boy in his arms, a smile broke over his face, and a far-away look came into his eyes. Was he seeing cricket-fields of the past, or dreaming dreams of the future – a future in which his grandson played a part?

Life had brought its ups-and-downs to Learie and Norma, but it had been mostly very good to them. The passing years had seen Learie gain recognition from various quarters. A Knighthood in 1962, the post of High Commissioner for Trinidad and Tobago in London in the same year, the honour of being made a Bencher of the Middle Temple in 1963, a Life Peerage in 1969! And always, standing by his side with the dignity that was naturally hers was Norma who, in the never to be forgotten past, having issued an alternative to Learie, "Cricket or me!" had yet known how to give in gracefully.

Trinidad, England, America, Australia, New Zealand, Ceylon, India! Far apart or near, they were yet linked in a closely-knit bond! So close indeed was that bond that even Death could not separate them for long. When in July 1971, Learie's innings on Earth was declared closed, Norma no longer cared for her seat in the pavilion. Two months later, on September 4th, she joined him. One newspaper correspondent, in paying tribute to her, quoted Sir Henry Wotton's well-known couplet:

"He first deceased, she for a little tried
To live without him, liked it not, and died."

But this runs ahead of our story by some years still!

14 His political career

"For the cause that lacks assistance, for the wrong
that needs resistance,
For the future in the distance, and the good
that I can do."

My Aim G. L. Banks

The year 1956 marked the beginning of a new phase in the life and career of Learie Constantine. It was in this year, which was to be a highly significant one for his fellow-countrymen as well, that he made a very important decision. He agreed that he would enter Trinidad Politics. The People's National Movement, under the direction of its gifted political leader, Dr Eric Williams, was then being formed. Meetings were taking place all over Trinidad and Tobago; while in the main centre, Port of Spain, week after week, large and enthusiastic crowds were overflowing what was soon to become known as the University of Woodford Square. It was evident that an entirely new spirit was in the air. As events were to prove, the long reign of the politicians of the colonial era was approaching its end, and only a few would be left to mourn their departure. In the changed Trinidad and Tobago that was coming into being, it was fitting that Learie should play his part.

Learie immediately identified himself with the growing national movement, inspiring many by his undoubted zeal and fervour. The organisers of the P.N.M. (as the new-born party was already fondly and familiarly being called) were, of course, fully aware of what his name and reputation would mean to the movement in the hard struggles that lay ahead. They knew that his prestige would be a valuable link, not only between the party and the ordinary citizen, but between the party and the outside world.

Learie, on his side, saw his entry into the political field as a means of even greater service to his countrymen. During the six years that followed, from 1956 to 1961, he was to serve them with all his ability, generously, and with absolutely no thought of self.

At a conference of the People's National Movement which was held on 15th January, 1956, Learie was elected the party's Chairman. This was the highest office in the party and was proof of how highly he was esteemed. The meeting came to a decision that there was need for a united effort on the part of all who were in sympathy with the movement. This need was an urgent one, as elections to the Colony's Legislative Council were only nine months away. The elections actually took place on 24th September, 1956 – the day before the forty-fifth birthday of the political leader, Dr Williams. Out of a total of twenty-four seats, the party obtained thirteen, some of which they won with large majorities. Learie contested and was successful in winning the Tunapuna seat. This seat had been considered a very difficult one to win. It was generally agreed that had the party put forward any candidate other than Learie, the seat would almost certainly have been lost.

Mr J. Hamilton Maurice, a former President of the Trinidad and Tobago Senate, was himself a fellow P.N.M. member, and he was one who supported this view. He commented, "As Chairman, Learie's influence was considerable in securing the goodwill and support of the people at public meetings and in winning their votes for P.N.M. at its first general elections in 1956.

"In General Elections there are cases where the party wins a seat for a candidate, who otherwise could not win.

"And there are also cases, more, where the candidate wins the seat for the party, which otherwise would have lost it. Learie was such a candidate."

This victory was to be only the first of many services Learie was to render the party and, eventually, the country as a whole. When the People's National Movement assumed the reins of government – thus beginning its long reign of power – Learie was appointed Minister of Works and Transport. This placed him at the head of one of the most important as well as largest spending departments in the entire administration. This Ministry, which is responsible for the roads and highways of the country, makes the person in charge, however, an easy target for criticism, informed and ill-informed. Learie also, unavoidably, came in for his share of criticism but, even now, it is sometimes forgotten that it was under his administration that two of the country's most extensive highways – the Lady Young Road and the Maracas Bay Extension Road – were opened.

During these vital years, apart from his ministerial duties, he devoted his energies to the important task of building up the party on a solid foundation. He was aware of the vast cleavages that existed in the society, the unwholesome relic of colonial days. Learie strove at all times to bridge the gaps that were hindering the growth of a truly national outlook. Some of these gaps were the product of interests that were not wholly of native origin. There was, for example, the attitude of the British-owned local press. This press had, for the most part, been hostile to the young and still untried national movement. Here, Learie's international prestige and influential contacts in Great Britain were to be of immense service. It was through his intervention that a definite improvement in the relations between press and party was established. He was of service to the party also in other and more tangible ways. Much of the financial assistance that the party began receiving from abroad was largely the result of his efforts. The name of Constantine was still a magnetic one.

During sessions of Parliament, his seat was usually next to the Head of the Government. His speeches, when he took part in the Parliamentary debates, were as a rule fluent, informed, and polished in their phrasing. Sometimes, they were spiced with wit and humour, but he could also be sarcastic at the expense of an opponent.

On Friday, 28th February, 1958, during the course of a 'No confidence' motion which was before the House, the Leader of the Opposition had attacked him. When the debate was resumed on the following Friday, Learie in his reply said in part:

"Last Friday the Leader of the Opposition said that I took this game of politics for bat and ball. I want to say that whatever reputation I have made, I have made it because of bat and ball. I have been to India, I have been to Ceylon, and I want to issue a challenge to the Leader of the Opposition. Let him land in India, his Mother Country, at any time; and let me land in India at any time, and compare the welcome that would be given to him in his Mother Country with the welcome that would be given to me. If he gets a better welcome than I, I shall pay some money into any charity he names. I have mixed with Dukes, with

Princes, with Kings and Queens because of my cricket; and I want to say that it is an indication of the mentality of the Opposition when they try to reduce one of England's greatest cultural games to a mere game of bat and ball."

Sir Learie Constantine takes his place at the London conference table for talks about Trinidad and Tobago independence in 1962

He was always proud of his honour and integrity as a sportsman, and on one occasion when these were assailed by the Parliamentary representative for the Tobago constituency, he made this reply,

"I am not going to say much except to remind him

that at one period I was a sportsman, that I moved around the five continents as a sportsman, and that I became respected by people in those five continents as a sportsman. I am accepted today in all five continents as a sportsman, as a man of integrity, and as a man of probity."

To Learie, politics was a duty as well as a privilege. From the outset, he won the respect of his colleagues and was looked up to as a Senior Cabinet Minister. He remained to the last a middle-of-the-road man, with a special gift for settling differences within the party or between the various Government departments, whenever they arose. This, indeed, was one of his most valuable qualities and gained for him the regard that is usually accorded to an umpire on the cricket field.

Yet, the fact must be faced that to some by no means unintelligent persons, Learie was not a success as a politician. Perhaps a good deal depends upon our definition of a politician. Someone who knew Learie intimately has stated,

"There was nothing crafty, cunning, or corrupt about his politics, which seem to be prevailing qualities of character to expect in many a politician today."

Perhaps the political 'game' is no longer a game that a gentleman can participate in and remain at the same time untainted. Learie Constantine was always the complete gentleman. Ever courteous, with an almost Victorian reverence for good manners, he sought at all times to avoid the "falsehood of extremes." It is perhaps unfortunate that he fell upon an age when "extremes" have become the normal pattern, especially where public affairs are concerned. This leaves very little room for the Constantines of this world to manoeuvre in, however lofty their principles. He was once asked by a fellow Minister how he managed to preserve his unruffled temper. To this he replied, "Is not a Minister allowed to be a gentleman?"

When Trinidad and Tobago achieved its independence on 31st August, 1962, Learie Constantine was appointed the nation's High Commissioner to London. This came as no surprise, as he was, indeed, the obvious choice. It was a proud moment for him and the members of his family. His appointment was welcomed in Britain also. He was not only well qualified for the office, but he was undoubtedly the West Indian public figure who was best known to the British people. Learie felt that he would be on familiar ground, and he did not anticipate any problems that would conflict with his duties or his status as a diplomat. In some cases, he was inclined, therefore, to brush aside mere matters of protocol, never doubting that he would receive the backing of his Government. In this he was mistaken, and affairs eventually reached a stage where he felt that he had no choice but to forward his resignation.

The complete story still remains somewhat veiled in mystery and one can only recount the facts as they were known to the public at the time. Learie had come forward and challenged the restrictions that had been placed by the British Government on West Indian immigration. He had pointed out that preferential treatment was being granted to Maltese immigrants.

Learie had also felt it his duty to intervene when a transport strike had taken place in Bristol, the white workers protesting against the appointment of a black Jamaican. Although the man was not a native of Trinidad, Learie had thought it wise to intervene. He knew that he stood well with British public opinion and felt that his point of view would be respected.

These incidents, however, led to a cooling off in

relationships between his Prime Minister and himself. Rumour also reached Learie's ears that Duncan Sandys, a British Cabinet Minister, who had passed through the Caribbean, had lodged a complaint that he was interfering in Britain's domestic affairs. Learie subsequently made his own inquiries among Governmental circles in Britain, and was informed that no such complaint had been made.

He was still not satisfied and resolved to travel to Trinidad with the object of explaining matters to the Prime Minister. His trip proved abortive as Dr Williams refused to see him. It was a heavy blow. He felt that his services were not appreciated, and it was this, more than anything else perhaps, that prompted him to send in his resignation. It is said that efforts were made in private to induce him to withdraw it, but he remained adamant. And so, in 1964, ended his political and diplomatic career in the service of his country – a career which had commenced in such a blaze of glory.

15 Britain honours Learie

"Above temptation, in a low estate,
And uncorrupted, ev'n among the great:
A safe companion, and an easy friend,
Unblam'd through life, lamented in thy end.
These are thy honours . . ."

On Mr Gay, in Westminster Abbey Alexander Pope

During Learie's long and distinguished career, he succeeded to a remarkable degree in winning the esteem and gaining the affections of the British people. It is no exaggeration to assert that his reputation among them was of such a nature that, in course of time, it became almost legendary. Also, his popularity, which remained evergreen, was not confined to any one section of the populace, but embraced people in all walks of life and in every sphere of activity. A truly remarkable achievement, especially for someone who set out on life's journey with no advantages of birth, racial origin, or educational background!

Britain's scroll of honour is a lengthy and memorable one, and unrolls, before the observer's gaze, a seemingly endless line of renowned and venerable names. It includes the names of statesmen and poets, soldiers and explorers, scientists and seamen, merchants and administrators, as well as the names of those who have distinguished themselves in the fields of law, medicine and sport. The name of Learie Nicholas Constantine is, by common consent, not the least on this proud and eminent line. To the British people – and it is, perhaps, the highest compliment that could be paid him – Learie Constantine remains one who came among them, saw, and conquered, nor, as is generally agreed, did he ever *stoop* to conquer!

The award of the M.B.E. (Member of the Order of the British Empire) which was bestowed upon him in 1946 was the first official recognition of his services. When the news broke, there was complete agreement that the honour was richly deserved, if we may judge by the comments not only in the United Kingdom but, indeed, throughout the West Indies. Despite his long and unavoidable absence from the Caribbean, his memory was still cherished there with warmth and affection by the very large number of fans who in the past had taken pride in his achievements.

It was the year 1947 when his welfare work in Britain terminated. In 1954, seven years later, he was called to the Bar. It was the realisation, even though belatedly, of another of his boyhood dreams.

Even higher honours were to come his way. It was in 1962 that a knighthood was conferred on him by the Queen. This was a significant year for his country as well, because it was in this year that Trinidad and Tobago achieved its independence. Sir Learie was appointed the new nation's first High Commissioner to the United Kingdom, a post which he occupied until 1964. It is interesting to note that his prestige stood so high at this time that when, in February 1964, Britain's Labour Prime Minister, the Rt Hon. Harold Wilson, was asked to nominate eight persons to be elevated to the House of Lords, Sir Learie's name headed the list. He had to wait a few years still for his life peerage, however, because certain constitutional problems stood in the way of its implementation.

These were undoubtedly crowded years for him. In

1965, he was made a member of Britain's Sports Council and, two years later, a member of the Race Relations Board. As a member of this Board, he rendered yeoman service in the cause of race relations which earned him the heartfelt gratitude of Britain's immigrant population. The British Home Secretary, Mr Reginald Maudling, described him as a "valuable member" of the Board and one who "enjoyed a very special place in the affection and respect of these islands". His labours in the field of broadcasting also, were not overlooked, for he was to be further honoured by being appointed a Governor of the British Broadcasting Corporation.

But what at the time afforded Sir Learie and Lady Constantine the greatest degree of pride and satisfaction, second only to the honour paid him when he was made a Freeman of the Borough of Nelson, was the flattering invitation to stand as a candidate for the Rectorship of St Andrew's University in Scotland – the University from which their daughter Gloria had graduated. The invitation came, in October 1967, from the Students' Representative Council of the University. After requesting a day's grace to consider the offer, Sir Learie signified his acceptance. His formal nomination took place on Friday, 27th October, a mere fourteen days before the election. In the days immediately following his nomination, there was a hectic period of activity on the part of his supporters. A brief description of some of the events, taken from a brochure published by the S.R.C. follows:

"On the Saturday before the election there was a 'Constantine' rally. Girls in green hula skirts and black sweaters molested people on street corners, eccentrically accompanied by a calypso band. Disciples, armed only with propaganda, invaded residences and preached to converted and unconverted alike. Someone in an orgy of enthusiasm, daubed 'Constantine green' triangles in prominent places over St Andrew's. . . . On the Thursday night, we held a hastily arranged torchlight procession. It all looked very fine. We were told that 'Constantine is mine every time' and exhorted to make him ours too.''

On the evening following the announcement of Sir Learie's victory, scores of enthusiastic supporters hurried to Campaign Headquarters to celebrate. Many of them had spent sleepless nights and their relief was tremendous. During the preceding days they had thought of little else, and now that victory had come, they were prepared to make a night of it.

The afternoon of Wednesday, 17th April, 1968, witnessed a most impressive ceremony when the new Rector was installed. Sir Learie, accompanied by his wife, arrived at St Andrew's early on Monday morning. After breakfasting, they were taken to University House where they met the Principal. This first day ended with a dinner at the Grange Inn.

The following morning they were welcomed by Peter Martin, President of the Students' Representative Council, who presented Sir Learie with an undergraduate gown. There followed various activities in which the students largely participated. Their next stop was the Town Hall for a meeting with the Provost and the St Andrew's Town Council. Meanwhile the bells of the Holy Trinity Church rang out loudly in welcome. Among the many places visited on that memorable day was Abbotsford, forever associated to lovers of literature, with Sir Walter Scott.

The University's Younger Hall was packed on the Wednesday afternoon for the formal installation of St Andrew's new Rector. Lady Constantine sat in the balcony with the wives of the other participants. Cameras clicked, as Principal Black of St Mary's College opened the proceedings. Deafening applause greeted Sir Learie on his entrance. He was accompanied by the three Honorary Graduates chosen by him for the occasion. They were men prominent, in various capacities, in public life – Sir Alec Douglas-Home, Colonel Sir Harold Paton Mitchell, and a fellow West Indian, Sir Philip Manderson Sherlock.

Sir Learie was introduced by Professor Butler, the Dean of Arts, who outlined his various achievements as administrator and diplomat. Now, he was to become the new Rector of this 'first university'. The S.R.C. brochure states at this point, "There was loud and prolonged applause as Sir Learie lost his undergraduate status and became a Doctor of Laws."

Sir Learie then repeated the Rectorial Oath, in which he promised solemnly to perform the duties and to uphold the traditions of the office. Donning the mediaeval gown which was handed to him, Sir Learie ascended the rostrum and addressed the gathering. He chose as his theme "Race in the world" and dealt in particular with the race problem as it affected Britain and her Commonwealth. At the conclusion of his address he received a standing ovation, and it was noticed that he and Lady Constantine were deeply moved. Well could they both have felt that this was one of their 'finest hours' indeed! No one regretted more than Sir Learie himself the fact that ill-health prevented him from carrying out his duties as Rector in the manner in which he might otherwise have done.

Her Majesty's New Year Awards for 1969 contained the name of a new Baron – Baron Constantine of Maraval in Trinidad and Tobago and of Nelson in the County Palatine of Lancaster.

Lord Constantine is introduced to the House of Lords by the Duke of Norfolk

It was with pleasure and pride that he accepted this long-awaited honour which symbolised, indeed, the crowning moment of his career. He considered it as an honour bestowed not merely on himself, but on all the other members of his race as well. The barriers were slowly but surely breaking down. It would also, he felt, provide another opportunity for service on his part. Yet he was well aware, conscious as he was of the trend of the times, that, among his own people in the West Indies, there would be criticism and scoffing remarks in some quarters. The following letter, written to his cousin Hubert Andrews, indicates this clearly.

11 Kendal Court
Shoot-up-Hill,
London N.W.2
12th April 1969.

My dear Hubert.

I was glad to have your letter and Card congratulating me on the New Year Honours. I am sorry that my continued illness prevented an earlier reply for which I hope you will forgive me. I must report however that I am much better and will soon be out and about again.

It was good to have your congratulations especially as so many of my countrymen would be jealous and critical, feeling as they do that I am a black-white man. I am proud of the honour and feel that this is another opportunity to serve my countrymen.

Norma is well and begs me to say hello to you and family and to thank you all for the kind thoughts and sentiments in your Card and letter.

very sincerely
Learie

Certainly a prophet is not without honour save in his own country!

A story which illustrates what Constantine meant to the ordinary man and woman in Britain is related by the Speaker of the Trinidad and Tobago House of Representatives, Mr C. A. Thomasos.

Mr Thomasos was at the time in London on Parliamentary business, and Sir Learie (as he then was) had a luncheon engagement with him at the hotel where he was staying.

Having to leave the hotel for a moment, Mr Thomasos left a message at the desk for his guest in the event of Sir Learie arriving before his return. The Speaker states that he has never forgotten the intense interest and excitement that was created when the identity of his expected visitor became known. On Sir Learie's arrival, there was an almost total interruption in the ordinary routine of the hotel, as practically the entire staff endeavoured to obtain a glimpse of the great man or to pay him their respects.

Mr Thomasos adds that this particular incident, occurring as it did in the capital of the Commonwealth itself, made him realise, more than he had ever done before, exactly what the name and reputation of Learie Constantine signified.

When we survey Learie's long record of service and reflect upon the honours it brought him, we cannot fail to find in his career a deep and abiding source of inspiration.

The poet, Alexander Pope, has written,

"Honour and shame from no condition rise."

Learie might fittingly have repeated the concluding line of the couplet:

"Act well your part, there all the honour lies."

16 This is your life

I have fought my fight, I have lived my life,
I have drunk my share of wine;
From Trier to Coln there was never a knight
Led a merrier life than mine.

The Knight's Leap Charles Kingsley

Learie entered the darkened cinema at Shepherd's Bush in the company of John Dalziel, and was led to a seat by an usherette carrying a torch. A film was in progress. He didn't like the idea of being late, particularly as the film was about Trinidad, and he had been asked by the B.B.C. to write a commentary on it. It had been arranged that John would come in a car to pick him up to take him to the cinema, but John, who had arrived late in the first instance, had insisted that they should have a drink together before reaching the cinema.

"Here you are, Sir!" said the usherette, as she indicated where Learie should sit.

Learie hoped that he hadn't missed very much of the film.

From the position which he had taken up close to Learie's seat, Eamonn Andrews of the B.B.C. called out, "Stop the film, please!"

The lights in the cinema came up, and laughingly, Eamonn turned to Learie.

"Forgive me for interrupting the film you've come specially to see," he said, "but you've been shown into the wrong seat. We have a chair reserved for you up there on our stage – for tonight, Sir Learie Constantine, M.B.E. – THIS IS YOUR LIFE."

Learie's mouth fell open in surprise. Then "My life?" he said incredulously.

Inviting him to see the film had all been part of a big ruse to get Learie to the cinema without his suspecting the real reason for his being there.

The audience applauded as Eamonn Andrews took him by the hand and led him on stage.

One of the finest tributes which the B.B.C. can pay to an individual is to feature him on a programme called 'This Is Your Life'.

This is Your Life: *Eamon Andrews talks to Sir Learie Constantine and his wife*

The greatest secrecy surrounds the arrangements made for the programme. Persons who have been close to the individual, or who have played a significant part in his life, are brought together from the ends of the earth, if need be, for the occasion.

In Learie's case, his wife Norma was there. So too, were his daughter Gloria, and his brother Elias, both flown specially from Trinidad for the occasion; Bessie Braddock, the Member of Parliament for Liverpool, John Kirk from Nelson, Winifred Atwell, the famous Trinidad pianist, Betty Snowball, well-known woman cricketer, Ian Peebles, former England cricketer and one-time captain of Middlesex, Gene Lawrence and his Triniana Combo.

But Learie did not know that yet. They were all hidden behind the screen on stage. As each member of the group was brought forward, memories of the past came flooding back, and skilful questioning by Eamonn Andrews caused Learie to share that past with his audience.

"Cricketer, barrister, politician, and now High Commissioner in London for Trinidad and Tobago," announced Eamonn, "Learie Constantine is, perhaps, best remembered as being one of the world's greatest cricketers."

He turned to Learie. "But your life has by no means been confined entirely to the cricket field."

Eamonn went on to review the part of Learie's life which he had spent as a Welfare Officer in Liverpool.

"A well-known Member of Parliament and an old friend of yours can tell us more about your work at that time. And here she is," announced Eamonn, "Member of Parliament for the Exchange Division of Liverpool – Mrs Bessie Braddock!"

Bessie was a good friend of the family. Her father was a Welfare Officer and member of the Labour Party, like Constantine himself. Learie was delighted to see her. Bessie had the biggest handbag ever made, but she left it offstage, in case it might have caused comment.

Bessie described Learie as being the ideal man for the job in Liverpool, and paid tribute to his tact and steadying influence.

"If ever a man deserved to be officially recognised for his work, Learie Constantine did," she concluded.

Betty Snowball was at the time a Physical Education teacher who had been brought from a school somewhere in the North of England. She kept wicket for England, and had been coached by Learie, who always said that she hit the ball as hard as any man, and harder than most.

John Kirk, while at school, had been coached at cricket by Learie. They had grown close to each other, and John had learnt to depend on Learie's judgement, not only where cricket was concerned, but also in other important aspects of his life. On leaving school, he had turned to Learie for advice as to what career he should follow.

"Be a solicitor," suggested Learie, and so it was.

Learie introduced John to T. A. Higson, Senior, Chairman of the Lancashire County Cricket Club, and a successful Manchester solicitor. John had never forgotten the occasion. It was on the day that Hitler invaded Poland. Seven years passed, however, before John Kirk actually went into Higson's office, and in due course qualified as a solicitor.

Tommy Higson had played no little part in advising Learie in business matters during the Lancashire League years, and Learie was always grateful to him. Learie was sorry that Higson had died soon after the war, and so could not share in the joy of his success in other fields.

Winifred Atwell, the renowned pianist, was from Trinidad. Like Learie himself, she came from an old Tunapuna family, and they rejoiced together as only Trinidadians can.

At one stage of the programme, Dr Eric Williams, the Prime Minister of Trinidad and Tobago, was shown on film. He spoke about Learie's work for the People's National Movement Party; his time as a Minister, and the automatic choice of him as High Commissioner in London.

Dr Williams also expressed delight at Learie's receipt of a Knighthood, and stated that Trinidadians were in good hands in England.

He summed up Learie as a great all-rounder, a fine representative of the West Indies as a cricketer and as a statesman.

Gloria, Learie's daughter, and Elias, his brother, were among those who would never forget the occasion. It was John Dalziel who had telephoned from London to get from them more detailed information about Constantine.

Gloria at the time was the Senior Mistress at St George's College, a Government Secondary school at Barataria. She and Uncle Elias left Trinidad together on the same plane. The weather was 88 degrees; hot, sticky and uncomfortable. They were to change planes at New York, and continue their journey to London together.

Elias, however, ran into a snag. It was discovered that he did not have an American visa, so he and Gloria parted ways at the airport. She was put aboard a T.W.A. plane to continue her journey. He was hustled into the Immigration Room and kept under surveillance while the powers that be decided what should be done with him. Eventually he was put on board a Pan-American flight and allowed to continue his journey.

Strangely enough, he and Gloria arrived at Heathrow, London, at almost the same time. It was Saturday morning. The weather was cold, and they shivered as they awaited Lady Norma Constantine and the old coats which she had promised to bring for them. The transition from 88 degrees to 33 degrees was not exactly a West Indian's 'cup of tea'.

From the airport they were taken directly to the hotel where they were to stay. They had strict instructions that they were to avoid being seen. Nothing must happen to spoil the surprise which the BBC had so carefully prepared for Learie.

On Sunday afternoon all who were to appear on the programme met at the BBC. Lady Constantine had had to make some excuse to get away from the house without arousing her husband's suspicions that something unusual was going on. A friend, put up to the job, corroborated her story of an appointment.

Back to the hotel on Sunday night to keep out of sight until Monday morning when Gloria was allowed to go shopping. She just had to buy herself a new coat! The old 'junk' which was the only thing her mother could slip out unnoticed was hardly the thing for her to be seen in. The coat having been bought, it was back to the hotel once again for her!

At eleven o'clock on Monday morning the entire group was taken to the studio, and rehearsal for the evening's programme began. They rehearsed all day. Nothing was left to chance. They changed for the programme in the dressing-rooms, and waited for the show to begin.

Asked by Eamonn Andrews about the memories of his early married life, Learie recalled a time when his wife left him to take charge of their only child, Gloria, for a few days. She must have been around six years old at the time.

Mrs Constantine had carefully pressed and plaited Gloria's hair before leaving, and left him strict instructions as to how he should take care of it.

"Comb a little girl's hair? Never again," thought Learie. He certainly agreed with Gloria that when he was through with it, it was more matted than plaited!

He laughed heartily at the memory of the incident.

The audience enjoyed every moment of the evening.

"To end our programme," said Eamonn Andrews, when Gloria had left the stage, "what better tribute could we have than a salute from your own people delivered in the traditional West Indian way? So here is the Sir Learie Constantine Calypso. . . ."

Off-stage, the Combo started the introduction to the calypso.

"Specially written for you and sung by Gene Lawrence, the leader of the Triniana Combo," continued Eamonn. "But before he begins, let me say – Sir Learie Constantine, M.B.E. – THIS IS YOUR LIFE."

Eamonn Andrews handed to Learie the famous, big red book marked THIS IS YOUR LIFE – SIR LEARIE CONSTANTINE.

The real one which he was to keep in memory of this wonderful occasion was presented to him subsequently. In it were the various photographs taken on the stage that evening, and it was inscribed thus:

"This programme was pre-recorded on 25th March, 1963, and televised over the BBC nationwide network in the evening of Tuesday, 16th April, 1963. Your appearance before our cameras was made possible by the kind assistance of your wife Lady Norma Constantine."

On the very last page it read, "This book and the programme it represents are our tribute to your sportsmanship, statesmanship and zest for life shown in a career, which, having inspired young and old for 62 years, still holds promise of even greater things to come. Sir Learie Constantine, THIS IS YOUR LIFE."

17 Home from sea

> "This be the verse you grave for me:
> Here he lies where he longed to be.
> Home is the sailor, home from sea,
> And the hunter home from the hill."
>
> *Requiem* R. L. Stevenson

"One day I shall be old, and shall sit in the sun in Trinidad and tell stories of cricket, and watch their eyes grow rounder and rounder as they listen, as well they may. And when I finish up, and stretch, and get up and make ready to go indoors, I shall always end on the same note.

"If I had my time over again," I shall say, impressively, as I hobble slowly away, "I would be a professional cricketer again. I would do it all again. I would live over again my happy life of cricket in the sun."

These are the closing paragraphs of *Cricket in the Sun*. Always, he had looked forward to the time when, his cricketing days over, and his youth a thing of the past, he would sit and tell stories of what had been. But Learie never got that chance.

Early in 1971, he decided that the time had come for him to return to Trinidad to settle down. His doctor had advised him that the cold English weather was detrimental to his health. He must return to the sunshine of his native land.

For years he had suffered from hay fever. His eyes were often half-closed, and his nose blocked. He was forced to wear dark shades and to use inhalants. Later, he developed bronchitis, and the attacks became worse and worse. It was only in later years that it was discovered that he was allergic to the pollen from grass. Of all things!

His wife Norma herself had been ailing for a while, but no one knew for certain that this was so. She was more concerned about Learie's health than about anything else, and only her closest friends suspected that all was not well with her.

Learie's condition deteriorated, as the bronchial attacks became more and more frequent. Throughout the entire period of his illness, however, Norma, who was constantly by his side, at no time thought of death.

The end came unexpectedly on an early summer's day. It was on the 1st July, 1971. He died of a heart attack.

"Learie's death shocked me quite a lot," said Norma afterwards.

Dr the Rt Hon. Eric Williams, Prime Minister of Trinidad and Tobago, sent the following telegram to the family:

"Trinidad and Tobago has learned with grief of the death of one of its most distinguished citizens.

"Baron Constantine has earned a place in his country's history by his achievements as a cricketer, barrister, Government Minister, and as its first High Commissioner to the U.K.

"I wish to extend to you on behalf of the Government of Trinidad and Tobago, and on my own behalf, sincerest condolences in the hour of your grief."

The Government of Trinidad and Tobago also requested that the family permit a State Funeral to be given to the man who had served his country as a Diplomat.

Learie's daughter, Gloria, and her husband, André Valere went up to England to be with Lady Constantine and to bring the body back to Trinidad.

On Tuesday, 6th July, the BOAC aircraft touched down at Piarco airport. The simple coffin was taken from the aircraft by a contingent of the Trinidad and Tobago Regiment. They draped it in the national flag, and then handed it over to the undertakers who had come to take the coffin to Port of Spain.

At the airport to meet Lady Constantine were various Ministers of Government. Mr Kamaluddin Mohammed, Minister of West Indian Affairs, gently kissed the widow's cheek as she alighted. Mr Basil Pitt, Minister of National Security, Senator Francis Prevatt, Minister of Health and Local Government, The British High Commissioner, Mr Roland Hunt, and Learie's younger brother, Elias Constantine, were there also.

Lord Constantine had come home.

Many were the tributes which were paid to him by his admirers. Among them was the following which appeared in the *Trinidad Guardian* during the early days after his death:

"During the 1930s when Learie Constantine was in his heyday, a song was composed in his honour by, I believe, some Lancashire fan.

It used to be sung to the well-known tune of 'My Darling Clementine', and its opening stanza ran something like this:

> Up in Lankshire,
> Such a dankshire,
> Where it's seldom very fine,
> Lives a Test man,
> Indies' best man,
> And his name is Constantine.

The chorus followed in the usual fashion:

> Oh, my darling, oh, my darling,
> Oh, my darling Constantine . . .

That is as far as I remember, but there may be others among your readers to whom the words of the entire song are familiar."

This song serves clearly to indicate the sort of impact Learie had on his own generation. I find it difficult to convince the present generation – far too obsessed with statistics – of his greatness in cricket. But Learie Constantine, like W. G. Grace, cannot be judged by statistical records.

As Neville Cardus, writing of Grace, has stated somewhere, "Like Dr Johnson he endured not by reason of his works but by reason of his circumferential humanity."

This evoked response from a number of readers, but the following letter, received by the writer of the tribute two days after the appearance of the *Guardian* publication, is perhaps the one of greatest interest:

Dear Neville,

My uncle, Lionel Darmanie, who is in his eighties, read your letter to the *Guardian* about the late Lord Constantine, and immediately recalled a few verses written by the late C. S. Assee many years ago. My uncle has asked me to pass the words on to you for what they are worth.

> In the Indies where the wind is,
> And the breeze is blowing fine,
> There is a stroller who is a bowler,
> And his name is Constantine.
>
> What a figure, full of vigour,
> And he sends the ball down fine;
> 'That's a bumper,' said the umpire,
> 'It's approaching bodyline.'

How he gammoned Master Hammond,
Who was bowled for only nine;
What a riot when Massa Wyatt
Gave a catch to Constantine.

Chorus . . .
Oh, my darling, oh, my darling,
Oh, my darling Constantine;
Who can stick it at the wicket,
Face to face with Constantine?

There may be more verses, but these are all he could remember.

Yours truly,
John Encinas
18 Sorzano Street,
Arima

Judging by this letter, if the author of these verses is the same as the author of the verse of the original letter, then the words were penned, not by a Lancashire fan, but by a West Indian one – a Trinidad lawyer with an interest both in cricket and in rhyming. On the other hand, there might well have been two versions by two different composers.

Many other tributes to Constantine, after his death, made reference to his greatness, not only as a cricketer, but also in other aspects of his varied career, including that of champion of the coloured man.

Among the foreign newspapers that paid tribute to him were *The Times, The New York Times, The Financial Times, The Birmingham Post, The Daily Telegraph* and *The Evening Standard.* The local *Trinidad Guardian* and *Trinidad Express* also added their quota.

The English sportswriter, Neville Cardus, in *The Guardian* referred to Constantine as "a cricketer of his race and climate."

"Curiously enough," he continued, "he does not loom large statistically. . . . But he was altogether unpredictable, and in his periods of inspiration, absolutely original."

John Arlott, well-known poet, cricket correspondent and broadcaster, writing in *The Guardian* also, stated, "He talked easily and sincerely at a dinner-table or a microphone, and he sustained his own position, and that of all coloured people, with a dignity and an absence of rancour rarely equalled by his reactionary opponents. His pride in his knighthood and life peerage was for his people. . . ."

Wisden referred to Learie's fast bowling, fearless batting and electric agility in the field, stating that they "have never been equalled as a combination."

A tribute in the *Trinidad Express* read thus, "As a champion of coloured people he had few equals, for he was devoted and conscientious in his efforts to win dignity, status and respect for coloured people.

"He himself enjoyed the respect and admiration of the people of England, and held some of the highest offices in the country, usually reserved for high ranking English officials."

Sir Roy Wilson (acting Chairman of the Race Relations Board) said, "He was a truly great and truly lovable man. He came here as an immigrant and his many contributions to our society are a standing reproach to those who say that immigrants bring nothing but problems."

These are but a few of the many tributes paid to a man who, in fair weather and in foul, had "played the game".

The funeral of the late Lord Constantine took place on Thursday, 8th July, 1971, at the Cathedral of the Immaculate Conception, in Port of Spain. On Government buildings and on many offices throughout the territory, flags were flown at half-mast in his honour.

From eight o'clock in the morning of that day until twelve noon, the body lay in state at the Cathedral. The coffin was placed on three stools before the altar, and five members of the Trinidad and Tobago Regiment stood on guard, with heads bowed and bayonets held downwards.

Policemen and women kept order as thousands of people who had known or even just heard about him filed past the coffin to pay their last respects. Many of the pious knelt for a while to pray.

A few minutes after mid-day, the body was removed from the Cathedral and taken to a waiting hearse outside the entrance, to be conveyed to the Funeral Home. The people inside the church stood quietly as eight soldiers, walking in a slow march, bore the coffin away. The doors of the Cathedral were closed.

Later in the afternoon, curious onlookers and sympathetic ones lined the route along Tragarete Road, Park Street, Frederick Street and Independence Square, as the cortège made its way back to the Cathedral for the Funeral Mass.

Meanwhile, Lady Constantine and other members of the family, Cabinet Ministers, the Prime Minister, the Governor-General and his wife, and the rest of the congregation had taken their seats in the Cathedral. The pall bearers stood beside the gun carriage.

The service was conducted by His Grace, The Most Revd Anthony Pantin, Archbishop of Port of Spain, who referred to Lord Constantine as "a man who walked with kings without losing the common touch."

At the end of the service, a nineteen-gun salute was fired. The coffin was then placed in the hearse, and under escort, the procession left the Cathedral for the Arouca Roman Catholic Cemetery where the interment ceremonies were to take place. Again crowds lined the route.

Many persons who had been unable to attend the Funeral Mass at the Cathedral joined the procession on the way to Arouca. Half a mile from the Cemetery, the procession stopped. The coffin was transferred to the gun carriage, and the troops slow-marched to the entrance of the cemetery.

At the graveside the parish priest offered prayers for the repose of the soul of Learie Constantine. A volley was fired, and then the Last Post and the Reveille were sounded.

It was a touching moment. Tears, unashamed, fell from the eyes of many. Learie Nicholas Constantine, late Baron of Maraval in Trinidad and Tobago and of Nelson in the County Palatine of Lancaster, all-round cricketer, author, barrister, lecturer, politician, the first member of his race to take a seat in the House of Lords, had been laid to rest.

He was truly one of the most versatile men of modern times, a man to be remembered, a man of whom any nation might justly be proud. Posthumously, he was awarded the Trinity Cross – the highest award his country could confer on anyone.

Appendix

For those persons who are interested in the figures, the following details of Constantine's Test Record are added:

Test Record
Learie Constantine appeared in 18 Tests against England and Australia between the years 1928 and 1939. He captured 58 wickets, scored 641 runs, and took 28 catches. His best bowling performance was 9 for 122 against England, in the Third Test at Georgetown during the 1929–30 Tour.

Overall Averages
Tests 18; Innings 33; Runs 641
Versus England: Tests 13; Innings 23; Runs 569
Versus Australia: Tests 5; Innings 10; Runs 72
Highest score was 90 in the second Test of the 1934–35 series against England at the Queen's Park Oval.

Bowling

Overs	*Maidens*	*Runs*	*Wickets*	*Average*
578·3	125	1,746	58	30·01

Best bowling performance: 4 for 25 (16·3 overs) and 5 for 87 (40 overs) in the Third Test against England (1929–30) at Georgetown.

Constantine captured 5 wickets in an innings on two occasions, at Georgetown and at the Oval (5 for 75) in 1939. He took five and more wickets in a Test match on six occasions, all against England.

Career in First-Class Cricket

Seasons	*Inns.*	*N.O.*	*Runs*	*H.S.*	*Avge.*	*100s*	*Runs*	*Wkts.*	*Avge.*
1921–22	2	0	24	24	12·00	—	44	2	22·00
1922–23	4	0	58	17	14·50	—	109	4	27·25
1923	31	4	425	77	15·74	—	809	37	21·86
1923–24	4	0	38	25	9·50	—	109	12	9·08
1924–25	4	0	37	36	9·25	—	48	0	—
1925–26	8	1	99	29	14·14	—	284	12	23·66
1926–27	2	0	24	13	12·00	—	211	3	70·33
1927–28	4	0	135	63	33·75	—	202	11	18·36
1928	43	3	1381	130	34·52	3	2456	107	22·95
1928–29	5	0	224	133	44·80	1	309	21	14·71
1929–30	10	0	150	58	15·00	—	572	21	27·23
1930–31 (Aust)	23	0	708	100	30·78	1	950	47	20·21
1933	9	0	181	64	20·11	—	310	14	22·14
1934–35	9	0	296	90	32·88	—	344	25	13·76
1938–39	2	0	12	11	6·00	—	69	4	17·25
1939	32	3	614	79	21·17	—	1831	103	17·77
1945	2	0	45	40	22·50	—	80	1	80·00
	194	11	4451	133	24·32	5	8737	424	20·60

Debut Match	Trinidad v. Barbados	Port of Spain 1921
Highest Score	133 v. Barbados	Port of Spain 1929
Best Bowling	8–38 v. Barbados	Bridgetown 1924
'Hat Trick'	West Indies v. Northamptonshire	Northampton 1928

Those are the figures! The facts, however, are that no cricket figures can truly reflect the greatness of Learie Nicholas Constantine.